For we wrestle not against flesh and blood, but against principalities, against powers, against the rulers of the darkness of this world, against spiritual wickedness in high places (Ephesians 6:12).

This book is addressed not only to Americanists everywhere, but to all Americans who love their country and who are determined to preserve its blessings for future generations. It is our hope that the book may be helpful not only in arming active Americanists with information heretofore unavailable, but also in awakening those good Americans who are still slumbering. Some of the latter who happen upon this book may, we hope, be sufficiently intrigued by our apparently "paranoid" obsession with "The Conspiracy" to investigate for themselves, become "paranoid" themselves, and join our obsessed army fighting for freedom.

Those who have arrayed themselves in the United States against the forces of collectivism have had to face a multitude of attacks and overcome many obstacles. In most cases it has been quite easy to demonstrate that these hindrances have been engineered and executed by the Collectivist Conspiracy, but such a demonstration has been lacking in the case of one of the most serious of all such hindrances, religious neutralism. It is our thesis that this obstacle, like so many others, has been arranged by conspiratorial forces who have perverted and promoted a religious doctrine for this very purpose.

Although the nature of the subject demands that religion be discussed, it certainly is not the purpose of this book to promote any particular religious doctrine. If such were the purpose, the book would emphasize the much more basic aspects of Christianity, not the fringe question which has, in our opinion, been perverted into a weapon of the Collectivists. The crucial question in Christianity is where the soul of each individual will spend eternity, not the details of what may or may not happen here on earth in the near or distant future. Our sole purpose in writing this book has been to help stem the tide against the forces of evil, which most veteran Americanists have come to recognize as Satanically inspired.

The views and opinions expressed in this book are those of the author, who is a member of The John Birch Society but who never has been employed by the Society and is not an authorized spokesman for the Society. These views and opinions are not to be construed as expressing any policy or views of The John Birch Society.

The author wishes to acknowledge the valuable assistance of the following persons who reviewed the manuscript and made many helpful suggestions which have been incorporated into the text: Mrs. Miles Butcher and Mrs. J. H. Fann of Chattanooga, Tenn.; Mr. Delmar Dennis of Pigeon Forge, Tenn.; Mr. Ned Dunn of Morgan, Ga.; and Dr. and Mrs. Robert Hall of Jackson, Tenn.

The author also is deeply indebted to Mr. Delmar Dennis for his valuable introduction, and to Mr. Tom Stone, Mr. Ed Curtis, and Kathy Johnstone for their indispensable assistance in getting the book published.

* An Americanist is defined as a citizen of any country who works positively. and aggressively to promote individual freedom and responsibility, using only those means which are moral, legal, and ethical. He is opposed everywhere by the Collectivist, who works aggressively, using any and all expedient means, to increase the power of a conspiratorial clique of Insiders whose goal is to enslave the world.

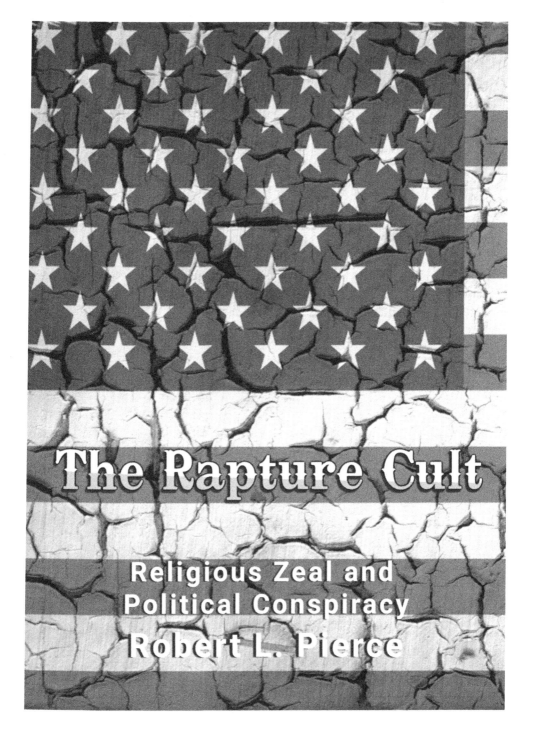

The Rapture Cult

Religious Zeal and Political Conspiracy

Robert L. Pierce

Independently Published
Amazon/Kindle
ISBN: 9798396734456

Robert L. Pierce

2st Edition/1st Publisher Unknown, No ISBN.

Homesteader Press, Compiler

Marcus Strickland, Cover Designer

INTRODUCTION

"Where the battle rages, there the loyalty of the soldier is proved, and to be steady on all the battlefield besides, is mere flight and disgrace if he flinches at that point." Martin Luther

"The Communists have always proceeded on the age-old theory that the most important accomplishment in all forms of warfare is to paralyze your enemy's will to resist before coming to actual hostilities. There is no surer nor more deadly form of paralysis to inflict on their enemies than religious neutralism. This is most convincingly indicated by the fact that at least two million Christians today, in the United States alone, have swallowed all or some of the British-Israel line for Protestants, or of the parallel line which is a more recent development among Catholics.

"These are the very people who should be most faithful and determined in their resistance to Communism. Instead they have been almost completely neutralized by a now gigantic scheme which the Communists themselves have been skillfully promoting for over a hundred years."

When Mr. Robert Welch penned those words for The John Birch Society Bulletin for April, 1972, I already had the assignment in addition to my other Major Coordinator duties for The Society to write an essay tactfully exposing this gigantic scheme of which Mr. Welch spoke. Subsequently, "THE WILL AND WAY TO WIN," both in cassette recording and booklet form was made available, but the attrition rate continued to worsen.

Now Bob Pierce's book has appeared, independently of The John Birch Society, with sufficient potential to immunize all those who have not yet caught the "prayer only" or "end-of-time" virus, but only if it's read and digested. What's in store for you, dear reader, is strong meat and unfamiliar fare. The recipe has been with us, as Mr. Welch indicates, for over a hundred years. Now you can see what this dish of conspiratorial pudding looks like. The proof is in the tasting.

TABLE OF CONTENTS

CHAPTER 1

SOME STAND AND SOME DESERT

"There are forces in the United States working against us. ...They must be publicly whipped, subjected to the torments of Hell!"
Nikita Khrushchev, 1959

This book assumes you know about the Conspiracy.* We don't assume you're an expert on the subject, but we do assume that you have a basic understanding. You understand that a conspiracy is, by definition, a combination of persons working in secret for an evil or unlawful purpose. You know that the rulers of the Great Conspiracy intend to enslave the world, that they wield influence or control to varying degrees in every country of the world, and certainly to a high degree in the United States. You understand the extreme danger the Conspiracy presents not only to your own freedom but to the very existence of western civilization. You understand the problem.

If you have not had an opportunity to learn about the Conspiracy, we suggest you read the postscript at the end of this chapter.

You also understand the solution. You understand that a conspiracy, by definition, must depend for its existence and effectiveness upon secrecy and deception. You understand that any conspiracy, no matter how large and entrenched it may be, can be destroyed by sufficient exposure. You understand that the way to destroy the Conspiracy, and to save American freedom, is simple but not easy. In its two hundred years of existence, the Conspiracy never has been able to maintain absolute secrecy. In many times and places, individuals of conscience and character have learned about various aspects of the Conspiracy and have exposed them to the light of day. From John Robison, who in 1798 published the book, "Proofs of a Conspiracy," [1] (a book read, incidentally, by George Washington)* to Senator Joseph McCarthy in the 1950's, most of these individuals acted essentially alone in their efforts to combat this evil. While their efforts were heroic and in some cases effective, and while overall they have provided us with a mountain of information about the Conspiracy, still none of them was able to expose the Conspiracy sufficiently to destroy it, or even to slow it down more than temporarily.

*On Sept. 25, 1798, Washington wrote as follows to the Rev. G. W. Snyder, who had sent Washington a copy of Robison's book: "I have heard much of the nefarious, and dangerous plan, and doctrines of the Illuminati, but never saw the book until you were pleased to send it to me." Again, on Oct. 24, 1798, Washington wrote: "It was not my intention to doubt that, the Doctrines of the Illuminati, and principles of Jacobinism had not spread in the United States. On the contrary, no one is more truly satisfied of this fact than I am. The idea that I meant to convey, was, that I did not believe that the Lodges of Free Masons in this country had, as Societies, endeavored to propagate the diabolical tenets of the first, or pernicious principles of the latter (if they are susceptible of separation). That Individuals of them may have done it, or that the founder, or instrument employed to found, the Democratic Societies in the United States, may have had these objects; and actually had a separation of the People from their Government in view, is too evident to be questioned." [2]

During the twentieth century many people, realizing the danger, have recognized the need for organization and concerted action, and dozens of "conservative" and "anti-Communist" organizations have been formed. Many have foundered on human weaknesses, or have succumbed to systematic attacks from the Conspiracy, which always has recognized and practiced the truism that the best defense is a good offense. Some organizations have survived but accomplished little. A few have survived and made significant progress.

In the late 1950's many knowledgeable persons were of the opinion that the Conspiracy's schedule called for achieving complete control of the United States, and thereby of the entire world, by the early 1970's. [3] The goal of the Conspiracy appeared to be to establish firmly its "New World Order" by its two-hundredth anniversary, May 1, 1976. Obviously the goal was not achieved. Although many factors may have been involved in this providential development, it is this author's firm opinion that one of the chief factors has been the existence and success, since its founding in late 1958, of The John Birch Society. This opinion is based not only upon the accomplishments of the Society, but also upon the nature and volume of the opposition directed against it.

In late 1960, instructions emanating from a Congress of the Communist parties of the world, meeting in Moscow, ordered the Communist Party USA and its satellites to initiate a strong attack upon the renewed anti-Communist movement in the United States. The brunt of this attack was borne by The John Birch Society."

In February, 1961 and continuing throughout that year, Americans suddenly were bombarded with "information" about a "fascist", "antisemitic", "anti-Negro", "anti-Catholic", anti-just-about-everything good organization called The John Birch Society, which most Americans never had heard of until then. The bombardment alternated between the theme that the Society was dangerous to "democracy" and the theme that it was a collection of ridiculous but harmless ignoramuses. The recipient could take his choice between these two ideas, but was not to realize that they were mutually contradictory. Many Americans swallowed the bait. But from the Conspiracy's standpoint the propaganda had one serious flaw-it emanated almost entirely from recognizable left-wing sources. Many Americans, recognizing this, surmised correctly that an organization engendering such vitriol from such sources must be good. They investigated for themselves and became members.

In early 1962 the Conspiracy, recognizing its mistake, changed tactics. Now the attack came from what had been built up over the years in the public mind as "responsibly conservative" individuals and publications. The theme now was that most John Birchers were well-intentioned, good people, but that they were being mis-led into irresponsible activities by that irresponsible ogre, Robert Welch. The verbal shelling centered on Mr. Welch, and the effort was not only to discourage patriots from joining the Society, but also to encourage existing members to drop out. The former objective met with some success, but the latter with hardly any. If anything, the effect was to confirm

Birchers in their admiration and support for Robert Welch. In the politically turbulent year 1964, the Conspiracy returned briefly to its original propaganda line, but this time it backfired even worse than before. Conservatives supporting Barry Goldwater were influenced by the thousands to join the Society because of the obviously false attacks directed at the Society from the Left.

Since the mid-1960's the propaganda line has been more subtle. Mostly the "news" media have been completely silent about the Society, breaking the silence only occasionally for stories about how the Society was "going broke" or "disintegrating." The line has been to create the impression that the Society was no longer of any significance.

Propaganda in the "news" media was by no means the only obstacle faced by the Society. Throughout the years from 1961 to the present. The John Birch Society has weathered a continuous gale of "dirty tricks" far more vicious and extensive than those which wrecked the aspirations of "Tricky Dick!" included, among a host of other forms of harassment, were well-executed whispering campaigns to the effect that the Society is a Communist organization.

It would be untrue to say that the Society was not hurt by all this opposition, but, in spite of it all, the Society continued to reach good patriotic Americans and to turn them into informed fighters for America. Birchers refined their techniques and tools by experience and built a core of battle-hardened veterans whose chests would be covered with combat ribbons if such awards were to be given out in this war for men's minds and loyalties. In the late 1970's The John Birch Society stands as one of the few remaining obstacles to the completion of the Conspiracy's world-wide slave empire.

In the early years of the Society, Robert Welch estimated that one million members would be required to achieve success, but after a few years' experience he revised his estimate downward to 400,000. It is this author's opinion, without the benefit of any inside information from Society headquarters, that, if the Society still retained as active members all those who have ever been active members, the 400,000 level would have been surpassed and the Conspiracy by now would be well on its way to oblivion. But obviously this is not the case, and this brings to mind the question of why many Birchers over the years have dropped out of the Society or, to put it in the military terms appropriate for an army battling for the survival of civilization, "Why have so many soldiers deserted?"

Not all have deserted, of course. A few literally have fought until they burned themselves out emotionally or physically, and can be termed truly to be casualties of the war. Others have grown old and are no longer capable of effective help. Some have died.

But many have deserted. Some, expecting that we could destroy in a few months a Conspiracy that has been entrenching itself for two hundred years, became discouraged because we did not win quickly. Others, failing to learn enough about the problem or the solution to become fully motivated, soon lost interest. Their attitude might be summarized in the phrase, with apologies to Patrick Henry, "Give me liberty or give me softball." Still others were too shallow in character or unequipped intellectually for the work which needed to be done. But many others were lured away by what Robert Welch has termed "the neutralizers."

In a pamphlet entitled "The Neutralizers" [5] published in 1963, Mr. Welch enumerated several ways in which Birchers were being distracted from effective opposition to the Conspiracy. He listed these as follows: (a) anti-Semitism being misled into believing that the Conspiracy is Jewish, and that all efforts are useless unless the Jews are attacked: (b) political neutralism-the pursuit of politics to the extent that all work toward exposing the Conspiracy is abandoned; (c) academic neutralism-becoming so involved in "ivory tower" ideological speculation that exposure of the Conspiracy is abandoned: (d) "tangentitis"-getting involved in tangential or minor issues to the point of losing sight of the main objective: (e) the "guns and groceries" syndrome-stocking up on basic necessities and fleeing to some supposed hideaway in the wilderness; (f) the "it's too late, all is lost" excuse for doing nothing; and (g) religious neutralism.

The extent to which agents of the Conspiracy have been active in promoting these neutralizers is of course impossible to determine, although examples are given in Mr. Welch's article where their presence is beyond question. Normal human frailties certainly are involved in all of them. But the controllers of the Conspiracy are, above all else, masters of human nature, experts at manipulating people through both their vices and their virtues. In view of all the other weapons directed by the Conspiracy against the Society over the years, it would be totally unrealistic to assume that the Conspiracy is uninvolved in some of the most serious obstacles the Society has faced in the past decade.

It is this author's opinion that the first six neutralizers, although still present, are no longer of major concern. The leadership and membership of the Society have matured to the extent that these neutralizers have been largely nullified. But the same cannot be said about religious neutralism. In the next chapter, let us look at a typical case of religious neutralism.

POSTSCRIPT

If you feel we're really paranoid about the existence of a conspiracy to rule the world, and about its threat to your freedom and ours, let us suggest that you're now in the position of a householder awakened at 3 a.m. by someone pounding on the door screaming, "Fire! your house is on fire!" The householder either can get up and investigate for himself or he can roll over and go back to sleep, admonishing the alarmist to stop disturbing the peace. If he investigates and finds no fire, he will have lost some sleep. If he goes back to sleep and there is truly a fire, he may lose his home and even his life. How sleepy are you? If you're willing to take the responsible course and investigate, we recommend the following, in approximately the order listed. All are available from, "American Opinion," Belmont, Mass. 02178.

CHAPTER 2

FROM INDIFFERENCE TO RESPONSIBILITY

"Seldom in history have so comparatively few people carried so heavy a load of responsibility, or met so mighty a challenge."
Robert Welch, 1968

Joe Goodbuddy is a composite not only of a number of people known personally to this author but also, unfortunately, of thousands of other American citizens. Ten years ago Joe was a typical carefree middle class American. Happily married, he was raising a young family, pursuing his career in which he made good money, and enjoying his money in his spare time. He scanned the local newspaper regularly. spending most of his time in the sports section but paying cursory attention to national and world events. He had an uneasy feeling something was wrong in his nation and the world, but he didn't let his vague concern interfere unduly with his enjoyment of television and his weekly golf or bowling. He and his wife were nominal members of one of the larger Protestant denominations, attending church regularly every Easter and Christmas, and whenever else it seemed convenient.

Then a friend of Joe's, a John Bircher, laid his hand on Joe's shoulder and began urging him to read. Reluctantly, just to humor his friend, Joe did. What he read was alarming enough to make him consent to view some films, which alarmed him even more. Over a period of months he came gradually and reluctantly to the conclusion that his friend the Bircher not only knew the horrible truth about the national and world scene, but also was engaged in a patriotic effort to rectify the situation. Joe recognized his moral responsibility to do likewise and joined The John Birch Society.

Our newly-awakened Bircher continued his reading and learning. as every good Bircher should. As he began to arrive at a clearer understanding of the Conspiracy, his alarm and concern continued to increase, but so did his determination to fight the evil Conspiracy. He became a dedicated man. He dropped out of his civic club once he came to realize that, although the club did some good work, there were hundreds of Americans who would do that work for everyone who would undertake the much more difficult and more urgent task of saving American freedom. He stopped watching the boob tube. He spent less and less time on the golf course, dropped out of the bowling league, and recruited his wife into the Society. He and his wife began scheduling their activities more and more to fit the requirements of the fight to save America, as all good Birchers should.

One of the more unpleasant facts of life our new patriot learned was that he himself was helping to finance the work of the Conspiracy through his contributions to his church. The shock of this revelation, coupled with his growing realization that he needed God's help to be more effective in the struggle, led him to seek a different church, one not connected with the Conspiracy either through the corrupt National Council of Churches or otherwise.

To some newly-awakened patriots, the statement that Joe's church was connected with the Conspiracy may seem unduly harsh or unfounded. Could such a situation really exist, and if so how could it have been brought about? Let us examine the evidence about this in the next chapter.

CHAPTER 3

NEUTRALIZING THE OPPOSITION

"For if the trumpet give an uncertain sound, who shall prepare himself to the battle?" 1 Corinthians 14:8

The Conspiracy, since the day of its founding, has been the avowed and vicious enemy of all true religion. The persecution 'of true Christians in Communist countries, and the setting up of phony churches presided over by secret police agents disguised as church officials, are known to all reasonably-informed persons.[1]

In the "free world," where Conspiracy control is not yet complete enough to allow the use of police-state methods, the attack on religion is more subtle. Here the strategy, in line with the Conspiracy's overall strategy of patient gradualism, has been to infiltrate religious organizations, taking control of each, wherever possible, from the top down. As an increasing degree of control has been achieved by the Conspiracy in each such organization or group, the sequence of steps has been about as follows: (a) neutralization of the group to prevent any organized opposition to the Conspiracy by the group: (b) watering down of religious doctrine, gradually converting it to a thinly-disguised advocacy of materialistic socialism; and (c) using the organizational structure to advance the program of the Conspiracy.

In the United States, the Conspiracy's subversion of Protestant Christian churches began in the late nineteenth century. The subversion of the large Protestant denominations is well documented and well known to all informed patriots. For an excellent description of this revolting situation, plus many further references on the subject. the reader is referred to John Stormer's "None Dare Call It Treason," Chapter 7,[2] and to an article in the February, 1970 issue of "American Opinion" magazine entitled "Apostasy-The National Council of Churches." It must suffice here to say that, under the leadership of Walter Rauschenbusch and Harry F. Ward, Union Theological Seminary in New York City was made the fountainhead of subversion, training students who became the top leaders in most of the large Protestant denominations.

The enormous contribution of Harry F. Ward to this sickening accomplishment is summarized in, "None Dare Call It Treason," Dr. Harry F. Ward contributed the organizational and conspiratorial genius to the movement. Ward is an identified Communist. In 1908, he was the founder of the oldest, officially-cited Communist-front group in America, the Methodist Federation for Social Action. A year later, he played a part in organizing the Federal Council of Churches, forerunner of the present day, National Council of Churches... Identified under oath as a Communist by Benjamin Gitlow, first head of the Communist Party USA; Manning Johnson, one-time leader of the Party's Negro Section; and several others, Ward was branded as the "Red Dean" of the religious field before a committee of the U. S. Congress. Ward posed as a Methodist but for 25 years he infected hundreds of young ministers of all denominations with his blasphemous ideas as a professor of Christian Ethics at Union Theological Seminary. He also served at Boston School of Theology at Boston University."[4]

The 1908-1909 period, as we have just seen, marked the beginning of open activity by the Conspiracy among these church groups, although the seeds necessarily were sown years earlier. Today, in most of the large Protestant denominations, Step (a) has long since been accomplished. Step (b) is either complete or in the process of being completed, and Step (c) is well on its way. In most congregations, the so-called "social gospel" predominates over the historic Christian gospel of personal salvation. While the overwhelming majority of the members in these churches are completely loyal Americans, and while a minority are still sincerely dedicated to the cause of Christ, still the organizational structures they support with their time, energies and money have been taken over at the top in a manner so stealthy and so effective that most members are completely unaware of it. Those few, like our typical friend Joe Goodbuddy, who do become aware of it. soon find that the control of the Conspiracy within the organization is so pervasive that trying to fight it from within is completely futile. They soon go in search of another church.

Subversion of the Roman Catholic Church is much more difficult to document, but is nonetheless extremely serious. Roman Catholics who have become informed patriots certainly have no difficulty in recognizing the effects, even though they may have difficulty in producing documentary proof. Any Catholic who questions these assertions should study the great encyclicals of Pope Pius XI. (1857-1939), in which he said, "No man can be at the same time a sincere Catholic and a true Socialist"[5], and "Communism is intrinsically evil, and no one desiring to save Christian civilization may cooperate with it in any undertaking whatever."[6] "Then he should compare these admonitions and others with the actions of Pope John XXIII, Pope Paul VI. and many (but certainly not all) other current Church leaders. For a discussion of subversion within the Catholic Church, see "Communism and America's Churches" by Father Francis Fenton." [7]

Documentation concerning subversion of the Jewish faith is also difficult to obtain, but fortunately at least one excellent book is available. The reader is referred to "To Eliminate The Opiate," by Rabbi Marvin Antelman.[8] Rabbi Antelman* relates an astounding history of subversion of the Jewish faith begun in central Europe in the late eighteenth century and metastasized to the United States about the middle of the nineteenth century.

*Rabbi Antelman, as Chief Justice of the Supreme Rabbinic Court of America, presided over the formal excommunication of Henry Kissinger *from Judaism on June 20, 1976. See "The Review of the News" dated November 3, 1976.*

The subversion of Judaism was carried out by a Satanically-inspired cult of nominal Jews known as the Frankists, headed by one Jacob Frank (1726-1791). This cult professed to believe that salvation could be obtained either through purity or through sin. They chose the latter, indulging in (among other things) sexual orgies. The Frankists were admonished to appear to be other than what they really were, some pretending to become Christians and others Moslems, but the great majority pretended to be religious Jews. The latter, to quote Rabbi Antelman. "integrated themselves into the Jewish community. Despite the fact that they were all outwardly religious, they still cherished as their goal 'the annihilation of every religion and positive system of belief." [9] They concentrated their membership among the intellectual, social, and financial elite of the Jewish community.+

+ It is interesting to note that the Frankists antedated the Illuminati, having been in existence at least as early as 1759, while the Illuminati were formed in 1776. Since the two organizations were highly similar in their methods and objectives, it is intriguing to speculate whether the Illuminati were a subsidiary or a continuation of the Frankists, or whether both were subsidiaries of some higher inner circle of the Master Conspiracy. The last alternative seems to this author the most probable.

The first major move toward subverting Judaism was made by Frankist Carl Anton who, in 1776, organized the Biblical Destruction Group, "a closed circle of intellectuals whose main objective would be to destroy the Bible." [10] This self-perpetuating group, with the aid of its conspiratorial connections, infiltrated its way into positions of prestige in some of the leading universities of Central Europe and began what came to be known as the "higher criticism" movement. Stripped of its intellectual pretensions, the "higher criticism" movement has been nothing but a long-term chipping away, little by little, at the integrity of the Bible as the inspired Word of God, leading literally millions of both Jews and Christians to adopt or inherit a skeptical attitude toward the Bible. Its results have been devastating to Western Civilization.

In the early nineteenth century the Conspiracy (in the form of the League Of The Just, later known as the League of Communists), building upon the success of their Biblical Destruction Group, further subverted Judaism by splitting it into three parts, "Reform", "Conservative", and "Orthodox." [11] Both of the new branches of Judaism set up by the Conspiracy, "Reform" and "Conservative", were based upon the idea so assiduously developed by the Biblical Destruction Group that the Torah (ie., Scripture) was not the inspired Word of God, but only the writings of fallible men. The "Reform" group, in addition, made radical changes in ceremony and ritual, while the "Conservative" branch adhered to the traditional in this respect. Those Jews who remained true to the faith of their fathers were branded as "Orthodox", which was given the connotation of "backward", "unprogressive", or "reactionary."

Returning now to the early twentieth century, it is not difficult to understand how the subversion of the large Protestant denominations, founded as they were on a belief in the Bible, was made infinitely easier by the success of the Frankists' Biblical Destruction Group. This group, judging it by its fruits, was formed for the long-range purpose of aiding in the subversion of both Judaism and Protestant Christianity. Initiated two hundred years ago, this sinister project of the Conspiracy is still bearing its evil fruit today. Thus we can see how far-reaching and deeply laid are the plans and schemes of the Master Conspiracy. We left Joe Goodbuddy as he was leaving his Conspiracy-connected church. In the next chapter, let's see what happened to him then.

22

CHAPTER 4

TO THE TOP OF THE MOUNTAIN AND OVER THE CLIFF

"O wad some Pow'r the giftie gie us To see oursels as ithers see us!"
Robert Burns

Joe Goodbuddy, appalled and heartsick upon learning of the degree of Conspiracy influence and control within his church, went searching desperately for a church free of such influence. His search led him finally to a small but growing Bible-oriented independent church.

Joe never had owned a Bible except for the large family Bible, ensconced on a table in the living room but rarely opened. Since this Bible was inconveniently heavy and cumbersome for study purposes, Joe went shopping for one of more convenient size, but quickly became confused by the multitude of versions, translations, and paraphrases offered in the stores. Upon consulting his new preacher, Joe was advised to obtain a Scofield Reference Bible, which he did.

As Joe attended his new church he soon was exposed to the doctrine that the evils he had come to recognize from his Birch education were in reality signs of the imminent Second Coming of Christ, and that it was useless for him to oppose these evils since the Second Coming would solve all earthly problems for Christians. He was urged to spend his entire spare time working for the church and winning souls, in preparation for the imminent "rapture of the saints." This was the term used to describe the anticipated secret return to earth of Christ, who would come to remove all true Christians from the earth prior to the terrible tribulation which was to follow. After a few months in his new church, Joe began to taper off on his Birch work. After about a year he decided to resign from the Society. writing a letter of resignation thanking the Society for what it had done for him, but explaining that he now was engaged in a much higher calling which demanded his full time and resources during the very short time remaining before the Second Coming of Christ.

Seven years later, Joe was still attending the same church. He was working harder than ever at his job, having expanded his business, and was making more money than ever. He had built a new home and furnished it with new furniture and appliances, presumably to await the Lord's coming in greater comfort. He kept up his insurance premiums. He was sending his two sons to college, where both were preparing for professional careers. As in his pre-Birch days, he was spending considerable amounts of time at the golf course in summer and at the bowling alley in winter. He had resumed watching the toob. In addition he had bought a new boat and was seen frequently on the lake, leading one irreverent observer to inquire whether he was as much a fisher of men as he was a fisher of fish.

Besides resuming all his old hobbies and recreational activities, Joe took up a new hobby, that of "rapture watching." He found that there were books to be read, TV programs to be watched, lectures to be attended, tapes to be heard, films to be seen, charts to be hung on his office wall, lapel buttons to be worn, and bumper stickers to be distributed, all promoting and reinforcing his newly-found idea that the Second Coming must inevitably occur soon. Joe subscribed to a newsletter published by a company known as "Second Coming, Inc.," which purported to keep him posted on how current developments in the news were fulfillments of Bible prophecy. He became an avid earthquake fan, combing each news report for supposed clues to the Second Advent. It could almost be said that Joe never missed an earthquake. Each of Joe's late-model cars bore a bumper sticker proclaiming, "In case of Rapture this car will be driverless." To anyone who has not yet encountered the "rapture cult," some of the foregoing may seem like gross exaggerations, but this author has personally encountered, or knows someone who has personally encountered, every one of these activities.

Joe Goodbuddy, encouraged by his Bircher friend to climb up out of the valley of ignorance, irresponsibility and inaction, had climbed laboriously until he had reached the top of the mountain of responsibility, only to plunge over the cliff on the far side into another chasm of irresponsibility known as "religious neutralism." He had lost his energizing realization of the danger. He had deserted the John Birch Society, without which he and his family might never have been led to Christ. Although he would never have admitted it aloud, he had in effect written off American freedom as not worth fighting for. even though he took advantage of that freedom in every activity of his daily life, including every time he attended a service at his church and most especially including those rare occasions when he really did try to win a soul to Christ. In Russia and Red China such activity is strictly forbidden and severely punished.

Joe's position, viewed from a logical standpoint, was completely ridiculous. On the one hand he was obsessed with the idea that he would at any moment be "raptured," which occurrence would conclude abruptly all his earthly activities and responsibilities. On the other hand, he continued to live as though not only his own life but also the lives of his children would proceed normally and reach normal endings. The only activity he abandoned was any effort to oppose the evil Conspiracy, which continued, patiently and gradually, arranging a life of slavery and horror for himself and his children while he played contentedly at his newly-discovered little game. Joe was hedging his bets concerning all contingencies of his life except one. Never considering that, if his religious assumptions should be wrong, he and his family might be subjected to torture and death in a Communist slave labor camp, he blithely threw all caution to the winds and gambled everything on his being "raptured" before things got really bad. Ignoring the warning given by the sufferings of Christians in Russia, China, Cuba, Poland and many other countries, who have had to undergo martyrdom for their faith, he assumed that he and his family would be exempt from such a fate.

Illogical and contradictory as Joe's position is, it is nevertheless the position today of thousands of former patriots, both men and women. If they had not deserted from the army and were still active members of The John Birch Society, they might easily make the difference between slavery and freedom for generations to come. Their actions could not have suited the needs of the Conspiracy better if the Conspiracy had been able to program them to react exactly as they did. Is it conceivable that they could indeed have been so programmed?

CHAPTER 5

"THERE ARE (ONLY) TWO SIDES TO EVERY QUESTION"

"For those with eyes to see, coincidences are clad in shining light."
Louis Pauwels

This chapter is a postulation on the part of the author of what may have occurred in the past. Consider the position of the Conspiracy Insiders in the nineteenth century, faced with the need to neutralize Christianity as a potential threat to their further advancement. They had made and set into motion their plans for subverting the large religious organizations from the top, and they felt confident that their apparatus could accomplish this in about a century. But they still had a problem.

In every field of activity in which the conspirators begin to make inroads they expect to encounter, and usually do encounter, opposition to their foul deeds. They term this opposition "reaction", and those who put up the opposition are called "reactionaries." Inevitably, in the field of religion, they knew they would encounter "reactionaries," those who, possessing strong faith combined with alertness, intelligence, and backbone, would not only be able to recognize rottenness when they saw it, but would have the courage and the ability to oppose it effectively. The problem of the Insiders was how to neutralize or control this opposition.

Having made a thorough study of their arch-enemy, Christianity, the Insiders were aware that the Bible states clearly that Christ will return. They knew also that throughout Christian history Christians have become obsessed from time to time with the idea that His return was imminent. One of the early cases of this is recorded by the Apostle Paul in his second letter to the Thessalonians, written about A.D. 52. The conspirators reasoned that, if conservative Christians could be induced to become obsessed again with this idea, their potential opposition to the Conspiracy could be largely neutralized. After all, it is a basic weakness of human nature to take the easy way out of our problems. If Christians, seeing their government being subverted, seeing their children being subjected to pornography, sex "education," drugs and permissiveness, seeing the institution of marriage being attacked by phony "women's liberation" and "gay liberation" movements, seeing a host of other evils all being promoted by one evil conspiracy if these Christians could be led to believe that all these problems were the inevitable pattern of the "last days" and were to be solved for them at any moment by the Second Coming of Christ, then many of them would feel relieved of any responsibility to oppose these evils themselves. Indeed, some would feel that such opposition would be tantamount to opposing God's will.

Having conceived this strategy, the Insiders cast about for means to put it into operation. The means selected was a psychological weapon used by them in many other fields, one which depends for its success upon the generally-accepted idea that "there are two sides to every question." To control the thinking of any group of people with regard to any particular question, usually it is necessary only to control which "two sides" are put forward for consideration.* Let us illustrate.

*This is a variation of the tactic which uses the fallacy of limited reply, as in, "Answer yes or no, have you stopped beating your grandmother?"

All informed patriots are well aware of the catastrophic effects of mammoth deficit spending by the Federal Government. Even relatively uninformed good Americans are aware of this. Why, then, does deficit spending continually worsen? Consider the alternatives presented in recent years for consideration by Congress and the American people. For Fiscal 1976, for example, the Democrat Congressional leadership favored a budget deficit of around 70 billion dollars, while the "penny pinching" Republican Ford Administration held out for a deficit of "only" 52 billion dollars. By constant repetition in the "news" media these were presented as the two alternatives, while the only sane alternative, a balanced budget with no deficit, was carefully ignored. This performance regarding federal spending is repeated year after year. During the Vietnam War, the two alternatives presented to the American people concerning conduct of the war were: (a) surrender to the Communists, otherwise known as "peace with honor," the course advocated by the "doves": (b) continuation of a no-win war, the alternative offered by the so-called "hawks." Winning the war, the only sane, pro-American alternative, was studiously ignored.

On the state and local levels the same technique is used repeatedly. For instance, the city fathers arrange for a referendum on whether or not to increase the local sales tax. The voters are told that they have a choice of (a) approving an increase in the sales tax or (b) having their property taxes increased. The sane, Americanist choice, cutting spending to operate within current revenues, never is mentioned in the propaganda accompanying the referendum. As a result, the increase in the sales tax usually is approved as the "lesser of the two evils."

Regarding the Conspiracy, the two choices offered to Americans are: (a) the concept of a Conspiracy to rule the world is ridiculous, and no "respectable" person will entertain such a thought; and (b) the Conspiracy to rule the world is so powerful and so deeply entrenched that all resistance to it is completely futile. This author has seen more than one American evade his responsibility by flip-flopping from (a), "no problem" to (b), "no hope", overnight.

This same ploy, with infinite variations, has been used over and over again on the American people for so long a time that it has become almost second nature for most Americans to accept one of the "two choices" offered them in any situation, without ever considering that there are almost always other and saner alternatives. The American people have been conditioned to accept, almost automatically, the proposition that there are two, and only two, sides to every question. Control over what "two sides" are presented on any question is achieved by seizing control of the applicable "tone setting" positions, whether it be on the national level by the Insiders of the Conspiracy or on the local level by a few venal individuals hungry for money or power. On the national level the "tone setters" include the leading politicians in Congress and the Administration, leading members of the federal bureaucracy, bellwether newspapers such as the New York "Times" and the Washington "Post", the news organizations of the three major networks, those who control what goes out over the wires of the Associated Press and United Press International, and the most prestigious nationally-syndicated columnists and commentators. On the local level the "tone setters" may be only a few politicians, a few leading members of the Chamber of Commerce, the editor of the local newspaper, and the preacher of the largest church in town. Whatever the case in a given situation, once the tone has been set, most people in the target population will hasten to fall into line with whatever has been established as "intellectually respectable" or "socially acceptable," shunning like the plague whatever thoughts have been placed, very subtly, "beyond the pale" or "out of bounds."

Now let us return to the Insiders setting up their strategy during the nineteenth century. To implement their plan, we postulate, they decided to establish the following "two choices" concerning the Bible: (a) the Bible is filled with errors, myths, and contradictions, and is not to be taken seriously by any intelligent, "modern" person; and (b) the Bible is the inspired Word of God and clearly teaches that the Second Coming of Christ is imminent. To be ignored and smothered to as great an extent as possible was (c) the Bible is the inspired Word of God and teaches, regarding the Second Coming of Christ, that no-one except God Himself knows when this is to occur. Choice (a), having been promoted already by the Conspiracy for many years through the "higher criticism" movement and by other means, would be used in the twentieth century as one of the means of destroying from within the large Protestant denominations. Choice (b) would be used to neutralize conservative Christians.

The "tone setters" who promoted choice (a) included Harry F. Ward and his disciples and spiritual descendants, as described in Chapter 3. The identities of the few "tone setters" necessary to establish choice (b) are unknown to this author, since the very nature of their undertaking provided them with camouflage next to impossible to penetrate, in most cases. Where any risk of exposure might exist, they could always fall back on Voltaire's dictum: "Speak your mind boldly, but when you strike, conceal your hand. You may be known; I am willing to believe there are people sufficiently keen-scented, but they will not be able to convict you." [1]

At many times throughout history there have been Christians who believed sincerely that they were living near the appointed time for the Second Coming of Christ. Many such groups and instances can be cited during the nineteenth and twentieth centuries as, for example, the group known as the Millerites who in 1844 donned white clothes and climbed into trees and onto rooftops on the appointed day, confident that the Lord was to return on that day.[2] Another group went through a similar experience in 1914, and again in 1918.[3] In 1922, the sect known as British Israel were expecting that the Second Advent would occur about 1935.[4] In 1975 a group in Arkansas quit their jobs, severed all connections with the outside world, and assembled in one house to await the Second Coming."[5] From at least as early as A.D. 52 there have been, many times, Christians who were obsessed with this wishful thinking.

Therefore, the task of the agents assigned to pervert, widen, and popularize this belief, and to obtain for it a seeming near-monopoly among conservative Christians, was not difficult. They had merely to find ways to encourage and twist a belief which some already accepted and which many more were eager to accept, since it promised instant relief from all their earthly problems and responsibilities. The technique for accomplishing this probably was identical to that used in many instances by the Conspiracy. No doubt it involved the placing of a few skilled agents in highly strategic positions where they could influence the thinking and guide the actions of thousands of innocent people, who had no conception that they were being used. These agents took no risk whatever of exposure, since they needed to pose only as ultra-sincere Christians promoting a particular point of view on what is, after all, a fringe question when considered in the context of Christian belief and doctrine as a whole. The point of view they espoused may not have originated with them. More than likely, they took an existing, relatively unknown, doctrine and guided its development along lines they considered most beneficial for their purposes. A few well-placed agents could have set the tone which has snowballed to become the overwhelmingly accepted belief among that segment of the population where it was most needed by the Conspiracy: ie., among those with the highest moral and religious values, those who, in the absence of such an obsession, would be in the forefront of the fight against the atheistic Conspiracy.

In this chapter we have hypothesized, from a knowledge of the aims and methods of the Conspiracy and from observations of current facts of life, what may have been done in the past. But does any evidence exist to support the postulate that a religious doctrine may have been developed, perverted, and popularized by a hidden force behind the scenes? Let us investigate.

CHAPTER 6

BORN IN SCOTLAND, REARED IN ENGLAND

"It is natural to man to indulge in the illusions of hope. We are apt to shut our eyes against a painful truth... Is this the part of wise men, engaged in a great and arduous struggle for liberty?"
Patrick Henry, 1775

A large portion of the Bible consists of prophecy, the foretelling. by writers inspired by God, of things which at the time of writing were still in the future. Much of this prophecy has been fulfilled, as in the case of the multitude of prophecies in the Old Testament foretelling not only the coming of Christ but also many details of His life on earth. Some Biblical prophecies remain unfulfilled, and a portion of these are concerned with Christ's return.

The Bible states clearly that Christ will return, and all Bible believing Christians are agreed upon this fact. But a wide variety of opinion exists among Christians concerning the details of His Second Coming. Broadly, there are in this regard three main categories of Christian thought. One group believes that Christ will return to earth to establish a literal political reign for one thousand years (the "millennium"). Since they believe that Christ will return before the "millennium" begins, they are known as "pre-millennialists." A second group believes that the return of Christ will occur at the conclusion of the "millennium," which they foresee as a thousand-year period of peace and prosperity on the earth, brought about by the eventual acceptance of Christianity by most of the earth's inhabitants. These are known as "post-millennialists." A third group believes that the "millennium" is a figurative symbol only, since the one chapter in the Bible in which it is mentioned is replete with symbolic language. Since they believe there will not be a literal "millennium", they are known as "a-millennialists." Within each of the three broad categories of thought are many subdivisions, and many differences of opinion concerning details. *Those who preach and promote the so-called "Social Gospel" claim they look forward to a "millennium" also. On closer examination, their "millennium" turns out to be a socialist world dictatorship.*

Most pre-millennialists believe that the future "millennium" will be preceded by a "tribulation", a time of great trouble and punishment for those who then inhabit the earth. Most post-millennialists and a-millenarists believe that this "tribulation" period already has occurred, most of them placing it during the very early centuries of Christianity when the Christians suffered severe persecution and martyrdom at the hands of the Roman Empire. Regarding their future "tribulation" the pre-millennialists are divided, some believing that Christians will remain upon the earth during the "tribulation" while others believe that the Christians will be taken from the earth prior to the "tribulation." Since this removal of Christians from the earth commonly is referred to as the "rapture of the saints", those who believe the "rapture" will occur after the "tribulation" are called "post-tribulation rapturists", while those who believe the "rapture" will occur before the "tribulation" are called "pre-tribulation rapturists."

Sound confusing? It is. But please hang on, and hopefully it will become less so. And it is important to the problem at hand.

In the history of Christianity, all of the above lines of thought have had their proponents for many centuries except for the "pre-tribulation rapturist" branch of the pre-millennialists. The idea of a pre-tribulation "rapture" can be traced back in history only to the year 1830. It is also important to note that the pre-tribulation "rapture" theory is the only one which foresees the Second Coming of Christ occurring in two stages, a secret first stage to take away ("rapture") the Christians, and a second stage which everyone will recognize. Observed over the long view of all Christian history, the pre-tribulation "rapture" theory is both a latecomer and a maverick. Nevertheless today, even though the doctrine is held by a minority of all those who profess Christ as their Savior, it is the one theory out of all those in existence which a newly-awakened American patriot is most likely to encounter. It is also the one theory out of all those extant which, if adopted by a Christian as his religious philosophy, all too often has a crippling effect upon his will to resist the Conspiracy. This crippling effect is brought about by three salient features of the theory: (a) the evils of our present day are held to be inevitable events leading up to the imminent "tribulation": (b) the Christian is promised escape ("rapture") from the "tribulation" by virtue of his being a Christian; and (c) the "rapture" must occur soon and may occur at any moment.

Since the pre-tribulation "rapture" theory is of such relatively recent origin, and is so different from all other doctrines held by Christians over a period of eighteen centuries, how and where did it originate, and how has it gained such apparent ascendancy in such a relatively short time?

To answer the first part of that question we need to go back in time to the year 1830 and in space to Scotland and a town in western Scotland known as Port Glasgow. There, in the spring of 1830, a religious furor developed about the Macdonald family, who were said to have worked miracles of healing and to be both speaking in "tongues" and interpreting the "tongues." The occurrences at the Macdonald home are recorded in a very interesting and readable book by Dave MacPherson entitled "The Incredible Cover-up," subtitled, "The True Story on the Pre-Trib Rapture." [1] MacPherson quotes at length from a book written in 1861 by the Rev. Robert Norton (1807-1883), a British physician and clergyman, entitled, "The Restoration of Apostles and Prophets: In the Catholic Apostolic Church." Norton, a member of the Catholic Apostolic Church and in full sympathy with the events he recorded, related how Margaret Macdonald, in the spring of 1830, had expressed her belief, which resulted from her study of the scriptures, that Christians would be "raptured" or "translated" from the earth prior to the "tribulation." Norton emphasized that Margaret's pronouncement was the first time anyone had distinguished two stages in the Second Coming of Christ, "for here we first see the distinction between that final stage of the Lord's coming, when every eye shall see Him, and his prior appearing in glory to them that look for him."[2]

Two religious sects in the British Isles took up Margaret Macdonald's new idea immediately, and with great enthusiasm. One was the Catholic Apostolic Church, headed by Edward Irving (1792-1834), a close associate and admirer of Samuel T. Coleridge, the eccentric poet. The first known promotion of the new doctrine in print was in the September, 1830 issue of Irving's periodical "The Morning Watch." Irving, a Presbyterian minister at the time, was subsequently expelled from the Presbyterian Church, at which time he formed the Catholic Apostolic Church. The services of this church were characterized by frequent interruptions by members "prophesying" or "speaking in tongues." It was their belief that, because of the imminent Second Coming of Christ, they had been empowered in the same manner as had been the very early Christians of the first century, as described in the Book of Acts and other places in the New Testament.

An early convert to Irving's new church was Robert Baxter of Doncaster, England. Of Baxter, MacPherson writes, "Baxter had gone down to London in the fall of 1831, visited some of the prayer meetings which preceded the manifestations in Irving's church, and soon was a regular attendant at Irving's services. He then became endowed with the prophetic utterances and had a number of personal revelations. Later, when certain prophecies made by him and others simply were not fulfilled, he became disillusioned and felt that he had been deceived and had in turn deceived others." [3] Baxter, in 1833, wrote a book about the

Irvingites in which he said: "There are some general characteristics in the work, which, apart from doctrines or instances of failure of predictions, cast suspicion upon it. One is the extreme secrecy enjoined by the spirit, and the manifest shrinking from public examination. The spirit has, both in England and Scotland, forbidden the writing down of utterances, and even the attempt to repeat them verbatim. Thus errors and contradictions are more easily concealed and explained away." [4] The chief financial supporter of Irving's movement was banker and politician Henry Drummond (1786-1860), the eldest son of a prominent London banker. Of Drummond the Encyclopedia Britannica says, "Meetings of those who sympathized with the views of Edward Irving were held for the study of prophecy at Drummond's seat, Albury Park, in Surrey; he contributed very liberally to the funds of the new church: and he became one of its leading office-bearers, visiting Scotland as an 'apostle' and being ordained as an 'angel' for that Kingdom." [5]

The other group to adopt Margaret Macdonald's new idea was the sect known as the Brethren or Plymouth Brethren, organized in the British Isles by John Nelson Darby (1800-1882). Darby was educated as a lawyer but became an Anglican priest in 1826, then left the Anglican Church to form his Brethren movement in 1830. The term "Plymouth" was applied to the Brethren by outsiders from the fact that the movement had its first significant growth in the town of Plymouth, England. Darby visited the Macdonald home in about the middle of the year 1830,[6] and first presented the new pre-tribulation "rapture" doctrine to the Brethren in late 1830 or early 1831. The new doctrine did not by any means receive unanimous acceptance. In fact it contributed, some years later, to the splitting off of a faction led by Benjamin Newton.

In his "The Roots of Fundamentalism", Ernest R. Sandeen, discussing the history of the Brethren, says: "Darby introduced into discussion at Powerscourt the ideas of a secret rapture of the church and of a parenthesis in prophetic fulfillment between the sixty-ninth and seventieth weeks of Daniel. These two concepts constituted the basic

tenets of the system of theology since referred to as dispensationalism..
Newton remembered, years later, opposing both positions. Commenting
upon Darby's interpretations of the seventy weeks of Daniel, Newton
remarked, "The secret rapture was bad enough, but this was worse." [7]

Darby, however, evidently was a dynamic leader, and his views
ultimately prevailed among his followers. Sandeen describes Darby as "a
man with magnetic, electric personal qualities combined with a tyrant's
will to lead and intolerance of criticism."[8] His following became quite
numerous in Great Britain and spread both to the continent of Europe
and to the United States. To quote MacPherson, "The two-stage coming
view of the Brethren spread to America and other parts of the world in
the latter part of the century. Darby visited the U. S. at least five times.
His dispensationalism became part of the Scofield Reference Bible
(1909). Darby died on April 29, 1882, at 81 years of age."[9]

What were the means by which Darby's doctrines were spread in the
United States, and how did they become incorporated into the extremely
influential Scofield Reference Bible?

CHAPTER 7

NURTURED TO MATURITY IN AMERICA

"The world turns aside to let any man pass who knows whither he is going."
David Starr Jordan

John Nelson Darby, during the period 1862 to 1877, spent nearly seven years residing in and traveling through the United States and Canada. [1] In the United States most of his work was confined to the cities of Detroit, Chicago, St. Louis, New York, and Boston, although on one occasion he traveled from Chicago to San Francisco and back on his way to and from New Zealand. [2] His earlier work in the United States consisted of attempts to win converts to his Brethren group from the membership of existing Protestant denominations, but this effort met with only limited success. By the early 1870's he seems to have shifted tactics, concentrating on promoting his ideas among leading clergymen and laymen in these churches without insisting that they leave their respective denominations. His success along these lines was greatest in St. Louis, Chicago, New York, and Boston." [3]

Two of Darby's most influential converts were James Hall Brookes. pastor of the Walnut Street Presbyterian Church in St. Louis, [4] and Adoniram Judson Gordon, pastor of the Clarendon Street Baptist Church in Boston. [5] These two men, while remaining in their established pastorates, became the leaders of the movement which was successful in spreading Darby's doctrines throughout the northeast and midwest during the last quarter of the century. [6] Darby's doctrines also had an impact on Dwight L. Moody, the famous Chicago evangelist, although

Moody appears to have accepted the doctrines slowly, and perhaps only partially.

The promotion of Darby's doctrines in America, by Americans, got underway effectively in 1875 with the establishment of a series of annual summer conferences. Beginning in a small way, the conferences expanded their membership and reach under the leadership of Dr. James H. Brookes and became semi-institutionalized as the Niagara Bible Conferences, meeting each summer from 1883 to 1897 at Niagaraon-the-Lake, Ontario. The conferences became highly successful in spreading Darby's doctrines to many influential American church leaders, especially those conservative leaders who were upset and concerned about the spread of the "higher criticism" movement in their churches.

It should be noted that the period we are covering here, the latter half of the nineteenth century, was also the period during which the "higher criticism" movement began to make itself felt among the Protestant churches of America. Beginning with the training of young ministers in the seminaries, the movement spread inexorably like a cancer through the body of American Protestantism, which became more and more polarized into "liberals", those who accepted the "higher criticism" of the Bible, and "conservatives", those who did not accept it but held to the traditional tenets of their faith. In this context Darby and his disciples made their appeal, which was always to the conservatives, since the Darbyites insisted, as did the conservatives, upon the inerrancy of the Bible as God's Word.

Although the Niagara Bible Conferences were initiated and dominated by those advocating Darby's pre-tribulation "rapture" theory. eventually many were brought into the conferences who would not accept the theory. It was disagreement over this doctrine that led to the discontinuance of the conferences after 1897, and to a split of the conference participants into two groups, a pro-Darby faction led by Arno

C. Gaebelein and Cyrus I. Scofield, and an anti-Darby faction led by Robert Cameron. The controversy, reminiscent of the earlier one in Britain between the followers of Darby and those of Newton (Chapter 6), raged for about five years and took on the nature of what Sandeen calls a "paper war." Each side controlled a periodical addressed to conservative Christians, and the "war" consisted largely of articles blasting each other in the pages of these publications. [7] When the "war" came to an end, it had become quite clear that the pro-Darby forces, led by Gaebelein and Scofield, had been victorious. As Sandeen explains, the anti-Darby forces lost control of the movement and, as their leadership died out with the passing years, few new recruits replaced them. The Gaebelein-Scofield forces, on the other hand, moved ahead aggressively, organizing new conferences promoting their point of view, and working toward the publication of the Scofield Reference Bible. Sandeen attributes the pro-Darby victory partially to superior organizational and editorial skills, but remarks, "Some other factor seems necessary to explain the relative success of the Darbyite dispensationalists at the beginning of the twentieth century." He finds a partial answer in the fact that many in the anti-Darby forces, deploring the controversy and disunity, simply retired from the field. He also points out that the pro-Darby doctrine is more appealing to the wishful thinking aspect of human nature. [8] Perhaps other forces also were at work.

Whatever the causes of their victory, the pro-Darby faction, headed by Arno C. Gaebelein and Cyrus I. Scofield, emerged from the "war" of 1897-1902 with an aggressive program aimed at widening their influence among conservative Christians. Since the conservatives were disorganized and lacked any dynamic leader, the pro-Darby faction, in succeeding years, became the "spokesmen" for "Protestant conservatism" and the "defenders" against the further encroachments of "liberalism. [9] "As might have been expected, their defense was largely ineffective since the very foundation of the Darbyite philosophy was a belief that all manifestations of the decay or degeneration of civilization were but further signs of the imminent return of Christ to "rapture" His saints. Those who whole-heartedly accepted the Darby doctrine were cheered rather than appalled by such manifestations. In succeeding decades the leadership of the Darbyites further consolidated their hold on the conservative wing of Protestantism, with the Scofield Bible serving as their primary source book. They have succeeded so well that, today, the truly conservative point of view has been nearly forced down George Orwell's memory hole [10] so far as public recognition of its existence is concerned. The term "fundamentalist" has replaced the term "conservative" in common usage, and the prime division within Protestant Christendom is now held in the public mind to be one between "liberals" and "fundamentalists", all the latter being Darbyite in doctrine. The "conservatives", those who accept neither the "higher criticism" of the Bible nor the Darbyite doctrine, are ignored completely.

By 1918 the Darbyite doctrine had spread in the United States to an extent that some Americans had become concerned about its possible effect upon the American war effort. Shirley Jackson Case, writing in the publication "Biblical World" in July, 1918, complained that "Premillenarianism is a serious menace to our democracy", it "throws up the sponge.... raises the white flag", is a "spiritual virus", and the "most helpless of all gospels." He observed that the Darbyites "lent themselves to the same purposes as the IWW [11] (International Workers of the World). An early example of religious neutralism stemming from the Darbyite doctrine is documented by Robert L. Spann in his unpublished manuscript entitled "The Achilles Heel of Conservatism." Referring to the controversy in 1933 about whether or not the United States should recognize the atheistic Communist regime of Soviet Russia, he indicates how the "liberal Christian" leadership promoted the pro-Communist line favoring recognition, while the "fundamentalist" leadership offered only weak token opposition: "The Christian Century and the World Tomorrow were among the most forthright church publications that urged diplomatic ties with the USSR. Most of the major Protestant religious leaders agreed. In February of 1933, 430 ministers signed a petition favoring recognition. The fundamentalist Moody Monthly thought the 'Second Coming' would solve the prickly problems of diplomacy: 'It may be, however, that our Lord shall come before such problems enter upon their serious solution, and thus many if not all of the readers will be spared the trouble of grappling with them." [12] This was an approach that was to be exploited by the Communists, and multitudes would be deceived by this conspiracy." [13] Informed patriots are aware, of course, of the crucial importance to the Conspiracy of American recognition in 1933 of the Communist government, which otherwise would have collapsed. [14] It was a significant turning point for the worse in world history, and religious neutralism appears to have played a part in determining the outcome.

Let us examine further the two men who emerged as "fundamentalist" leaders at the turn of the century. Arno C. Gaebelein (1861-1945) arrived in the United States as an immigrant from Germany in 1879 and became a minister in the German conference of the Methodist Church. He attended some of the Niagara conferences and became well acquainted with James H. Brookes, who commended Gaebelein and his work in Brookes' publication "Truth." [16] During the 1890's Gaebelein was engaged in evangelizing the Jews on the East Side of New York City.* As a result of his conversion to the Darbyite philosophy, Gaebelein decided in 1899 to leave the Methodist Church; later he gave up his Jewish mission work as well, to allow him to spend full time as leader of the Darbyite faction. Beginning in 1900 and continuing for more than thirty years, Gaebelein conducted a nation-wide campaign, traveling to nearly every state in the union as well as to most parts of Canada to hold meetings and conferences, generally of one week duration. He had no formal ties, during all this time, with any organized church, but conducted his work in each locality with the aid of any local church that would provide him facilities and an audience. [17] His impact in spreading the Darbyite doctrine across North America was tremendous. Gaebelein and Scofield apparently became close friends and colleagues sometime during the fifteen-year duration of the conferences at Niagara-on-the-Lake.

During the 1890's, waves of Jews were emigrating from Russia and settling on the Lower East Side of New York, as noted in a later chapter. After studying law in St. Louis, Scofield in 1880 was dispatched by the Cerre family to Atchison, Kansas to look after some Cerre financial interests there. Having been directed by the Cerre's to hire the best legal counsel available in Kansas, Scofield engaged John J. Ingalls, a prominent lawyer and politician. [18]

Cyrus Ingerson Scofield (1843-1921) was born in Michigan but was reared in Wilson County, Tennessee. Serving in the Confederate Army during the Civil War, he received the Confederate Cross of Honor for bravery at the Battle of Antietam. At the end of the war, Scofield went to live in St. Louis with his older sister, who had married into one of the prominent pioneer French families of that city. In 1866, Scofield married Helene Lebeau Cerre, a Roman Catholic and a member of another prominent old French family.

In succeeding years Scofield and Ingalls became law partners as well as political allies. Both became members of the Kansas State Legislature, where Scofield was instrumental in electing Ingalls to the United States Senate in 1872. Ingalls in turn succeeded, in 1873, in having Scofield appointed at age 30 as United States Attorney for the district of Kansas and the Indian Territory. [19] This rather remarkable appointment was made at a time when Federal officials were still punishing the South and white Southerners under "Reconstruction."

It is interesting to note the oath of office to which the decorated Confederate soldier "did solemnly swear" as he entered upon his duties as U. S. Attorney on June 9, 1873. He swore that he had 'never voluntarily borne arms against the United States since I have been a citizen thereof; that I have voluntarily given no aid, countenance, counsel, or encouragement to persons engaged in armed hostility thereto... that I have not yielded a voluntary support to any pretended government. authority, power or constitution, within the United States, hostile or inimical thereto." [20]

Scofield was not long in office. By December, 1873 he was being accused by Kansas newspapers of corruption in office, and on December 20th he submitted his resignation without stating the reason. [21] So far as we know, no public investigation or legal action resulting from the affair is recorded.*

The biography of Scofield written by his ardent admirer, Charles G. Trumbull approved by Scofield and published by the Oxford University Press, says that Scofield served as U.S. District Attorney for two years, although the records show clearly that he served only six months. Trumbull says that Scofield resigned his position because law was his chosen life work, and his political work was interfering with it. [22]

In 1879, at the age of 36, Scofield became a Christian and soon thereafter began studying in St. Louis under the previously mentioned Dr. James H. Brookes, one of the chief leaders of the Niagara Conferences. Arno C. Gaebelein, in his book about the writing of the Scofield Bible, relates that Scofield was able to learn from Brookes things that he could not have learned in any of the theological seminaries in America at that time. [23]

Scofield's record in Kansas was not easily forgotten. When, in 1881, the word reached Topeka that Scofield had become a Congregational minister, an article appeared in the Topeka "Daily Capital" of August 27 which began as follows: "Cyrus I. Scofield, formerly of Kansas, late lawyer, politician and shyster generally, has come to the surface again. The last personal knowledge that Kansans have had of this peer among scalawags, was when about four years ago, after a series of forgeries and confidence games he left the state and a destitute family and took refuge in Canada... nothing being heard of him until within the past two years when he turned up in St. Louis, where he had a wealthy widowed sister living who had generally come to the front and squared up Cyrus' little follies and foibles by paying good round sums of money." [24]

In 1882 Scofield became the pastor of the First Congregational Church in Dallas, Texas, where he remained until he transferred his work to Northfield, Mass. in 1895.

Scofield began work on his Reference Bible in 1903, after he and his friend Gaebelein had secured financial backing to enable Scofield to drop most of his pastoral duties and spend almost full time on the project. Some of his financial backers were: Lyman Stewart, president of the Union Oil Co. of California; [25] Francis E. Fitch, a member of the Plymouth Brethren and the head of a printing company which printed the New York Stock Exchange lists: [26] Alwyn Ball, Jr., a real estate broker and member of the large New York real estate firm of Southack and Ball;" [27] John B. Buss, a St. Louis businessman; [28] and John T. Pirie, owner and New York representative of Carson, Pirie, Scott & Co., the large Chicago department store. [29] Pirie owned a large estate at Sea Cliff on the north shore of Long Island, and it was there, in the summer of 1902, that the decision was made to proceed with the Reference Bible.

During the years he spent writing the Reference Bible, Scofield resided in a number of places. He first moved from East Northfield, Mass, back to Dallas, the scene of his first ministry, but in 1904 he decided to visit England and Montreux, Switzerland, where he remained for nine months. He returned to Dallas in 1905, but in 1906 we find him first in New York City and then in Ashuelot, New Hampshire, continuing the work. In the fall of 1906 he again left for Europe, remaining until the following summer. During his two trips abroad he lectured throughout the British Isles, as well as before English speaking audiences in Rome, Paris, and Berlin. He visited Palestine and studied in libraries at Oxford and in Geneva, Switzerland. In the summer of 1907 he was writing in Orion, Michigan. By the fall of 1908 he was living at 21 Fort Washington Ave., New York City. [30]

The Scofield Reference Bible was completed in 1908 and was published early in 1909 by none other than the Oxford University Press, one of the most prestigious publishers in the English-speaking world. Gaebelein relates how Scofield had met a Mr. Scott of the London publishing house of Morgan and Scott, and how, while the Reference Bible was being written, Scofield visited with Scott in England. To quote Gaebelein, "Mr. Scott said that his own firm would gladly undertake the publication, but he feared Morgan and Scott could not give to the Reference Bible the world-wide introduction it must have. He added. "There is only one publishing house which can handle your Reference Bible and that is the Oxford University Press. A few days later, Mr. Scott took Dr. Scofield to the office of Mr. Henry Frowde, the chief of the great Oxford University Press, which is so widely and favorably known throughout the English-speaking world. He became at once interested. [31]

The Scofield Bible is essentially a King James Version which has been interpreted and augmented by the addition of footnote commentaries written primarily by Cyrus Scofield, with advice and collaboration from seven consulting editors. One of these was Arno C. Gaebelein, whose field of expertise was prophecy. While the commentaries support orthodox Christian tenets in many respects, they promote, in every passage relevant to the question, the pre-tribulation "rapture" and related doctrines first espoused by Irving and Darby around the year 1830. Ernest R. Sandeen says of the Bible that it "combined an attractive format of typography, paragraphing, notes, and cross references with the theology of Darbyite dispensationalism. The book has thus been subtly but powerfully influential in spreading those views among hundreds of thousands who have regularly read that Bible and who often have been unaware of the distinction between the ancient text and the Scofield interpretation." [32]

In the nearly seven decades since its first publication, the Scofield Bible has been promoted to the extent that today, in many fundamentalist churches, it is nearly the only Bible accepted. It has had a profound influence upon the religious thinking of millions of American Christians, bringing the doctrines of Irving and Darby into nearly every crossroads hamlet in America.

It is interesting that another religious movement similar in many ways to the Darbyite movement has developed over approximately the same period of time, on a strikingly parallel path. This movement, known as "British Israel", is also having a strong neutralizing influence today. The doctrine of the British Israelites is that the British people are the descendants of the ten lost tribes of Israel, whose "destiny", as "God's chosen people", is to rule the world during the fast-approaching "millennium." This cult appears to have had its origin with an Englishman named Richard Brothers, who published in 1822 a book entitled "Correct Account of the Invasion of England by the Saxons, Showing the English Nation to be Descendants of the Lost Ten Tribes." During the year 1845 and the closely ensuing years, four additional books were published in England, detailing and enlarging the doctrine. These were "Our Israelitish Origin", "Israelites Found", "England, the Remnant of Judah", and "Our Inheritance In The Great Pyramid." In 1871 an additional book was published which sold 250,000 copies, and two magazines were started. By 1880 the movement had spread to the United States and Canada.

The British Israelites claim at least two million adherents and have a number of congregations in the United States and Canada, seldom if ever identified by the name "British Israel", but going under a variety of names. Their influence appears to be much more widespread than their numbers would indicate, since they make a concerted effort to insinuate their beliefs, in whole or in part, into the religious thinking of multitudes outside their immediate religious household. Today their primary means of disseminating their ideas is their radio program "The World Tomorrow", heard five days a week over hundreds of stations. Listeners who write in receive free copies of their attractively printed slick paper magazine, "Plain Truth."

The neutralizing effect of the British Israel message comes from its insistence that the evils of our day are inevitable developments. that nothing can or should be done to oppose them, but that those of Anglo-Saxon descent have no need to worry, since they will emerge as rulers of the world during the imminent "millennium." Anti-Semitism also is involved, since the British Israelites insist that today's Jews are not true Israelites, but only imposters. The British Israelites advocate the "Rule of Equity" which turns out, upon examination, to be a euphemism for socialism. They also advocate a world monetary system, world disarmament, and support of the United Nations. In spite of their advocacy of such left-wing causes, the tone of their propaganda is such that its main appeal is to the moral, conservative, patriotic individual with fundamental religious beliefs. British Israel propaganda is seldom identified with British Israel, but usually can be recognized by its frequent employment of such key words as "Kingdom". "David", and "destiny", and by its continual emphasis on "prophecy." [33]

Perhaps we should ask ourselves whether the influences we have discussed in this chapter have spread in America beyond the confines of fundamentalist Protestantism. Let's take a look.

CHAPTER 8

GROWN FAT, PROSPEROUS, AND INFLUENTIAL

"For my part, whatever anguish of spirit it may cost, I am willing to know the whole truth; to know the worst and to provide for it."
Patrick Henry, 1775
"Am I therefore become your enemy, because I tell you the truth?"
Galatians 4:16.

In the mid-1960's, when the author was a less experienced member of The John Birch Society, he was invited to a meeting at the home of a couple who were both very active members. The subject of the well-attended meeting was a lecture, by someone from out of town whose name has been forgotten, based upon Dr. Arno C. Gaebelein's book "The Conflict of the Ages." [1] The lecture was followed by a brisk sale of the book. Within a few months thereafter, several Birchers who had attended the meeting, including the host and hostess, had dropped out of the Society. Meanwhile, the out-of-town visitor probably had moved on to other performances in other cities. This was the author's first personal experience with religious neutralism.

"The Conflict of the Ages" contains much true information about the Conspiracy but, in the final chapters, promotes the pre-tribulation "rapture" doctrine. The book also quotes extensively from the "Protocols of the Learned Elders of Zion", presenting the notorious "Protocols" as a reliable source of information, [2] although informed Americanists are well aware that the "Protocols" are in fact an anti-Semitic forgery. [3] Thus Gaebelein's book manages to combine two neutralizers, anti-Semitism and religious neutralism.

Gaebelein comments that Nilus, the alleged Russian publisher of the "Protocols", must have been a devout believer in prophecy since the title page of his "Protocols" contains a number of Bible references which the Scofieldians use as parts of their "proof." [4] Since the main thrust of the "Protocols" is to blame the Jews for the evil accomplishments of the Conspiracy, it is logical to assume that the "Protocols" are themselves a work of the Conspiracy. It is intriguing, then, to learn that the "Protocols" themselves combine religious neutralism with anti-Semitism. Tracing the history of the "Protocols" is itself a fascinating pursuit, but is outside the scope of this book. One book known to the author which provides some highly interesting glimpses down this side road is "The Truth About the Protocols of Zion." [5]

Returning to the main road of our journey, let us examine other signs of the Scofieldian or British Israel influences in areas where they might not reasonably be expected. How about the channels of communication controlled by the Insiders? Hal Lindsey, a graduate of Dallas Theological Seminary, a prominent transmission belt for the Scofieldian doctrine,* and a professional exponent of the doctrine through his books and lectures, has entree to speak before huge audiences on the campuses of large "liberal" universities throughout the country. His book "The Late Great Planet Earth", first published in 1970, already had been reprinted nine times by March, 1971, and has been made into a film which is receiving wide promotion. Garner Ted Armstrong, the radio spokesman for British Israel, broadcasts the message continually over hundreds of radio stations. Unlike conservative broadcasters, he seems never to have any need for contributions to keep his program on the air, nor does he seem to suffer harassment from the FCC. Motion pictures such as "The Omen", a gory tale of horror purveying the doctrine, are produced by the movie industry and promoted at length on network television talk shows. Ninety-minute network television programs are devoted to interviewing expounders of the doctrine. [7]

*The founding of Dallas Theological Seminary in 1924 fulfilled one of C. I. Scofield's long-standing goals. [6]

Paperback books promoting the Scofieldian Doctrine abound at nearly every sales outlet. Any reader who questions this should examine the paperbacks on sale at his local supermarket, drug store, or airport, looking for titles such as "Armageddon". "Antichrist After the Omen", "The Last Days of Man", "Amazing Prophecies", "The Great Flying Saucer Myth", and of course the modern prototype of them all, "The Late Great Planet Earth." These titles are a mere sampling of those available. Such books have multiplied like cockroaches in the past few years, until their titles number in the scores. Neither is the college crowd neglected. "Comic" books are available which present the same message in simplified form for the victims of our "progressive" public education system. A sample title here is "There's a New World Coming", by none other than Hal Lindsey, author of "The Late Great Planet Earth."

As an example of what is found in these books, consider these thoughts excerpted from just one of them, "Armageddon-Oil and the Middle East Crisis" by John F. Walvoord, President of the Scofieldian Dallas Theological Seminary since 1952. [8] (a) The energy crisis is a problem (pp. 43-52); (b) pollution is a problem (p. 148); (c) over-population is a problem (p. 149); (d) mass starvation is a problem (p. 149); (e) economic instability is a problem (p. 135); (f) these problems demand the formation of a dictatorial world government as man's last hope (pp. 135 and 144); (g) Christians need not be concerned, because they will be "raptured" (p. 186); (h) current developments in the Middle East point to the "rapture" as the next dramatic and important event (p. 195); and (i) a checklist is provided for "rapture watchers" (pp. 200-204).

It may be surprising to some that these "religious" books appear in the same sales outlets, and often on the same bookracks, with the pornographic literature which has become almost the standard in the paperback industry. Informed Americanists should ask themselves why. Informed patriots should ask themselves whether Americanists could ever hope to get their message promoted on such a scale through such channels. Fundamental Christians should ask themselves why it is that this one particular aspect of their faith is proclaimed so widely throughout the land through media and institutions which many fundamentalists should recognize as hostile to true Christianity. Both patriots and fundamental Christians should reflect over the possible motives of those who bring such things to pass.

Looking at the other side of the coin, the few books available which contest the Scofieldian doctrine have tough going indeed in today's book market. Anyone questioning this should try to obtain MacPherson's "The Incredible Cover-Up" [9] at any religious bookstore which sells Scofieldian literature, as most of the Protestant-oriented stores do. Typically, you may be led to believe that MacPherson is a non-person and his book is a non-book.

The IP.S. has become even more notorious with the disclosures surrounding the murder of the Communist agent Orlando Letelier. See "The Review of the News" of April 27 and May 4, 1977, and "American Opinion" of May, 1977.

In the April, 1971 issue of "American Opinion" magazine, Gary Allen, writing about the "think tanks" in America, told how the "think tank" known as the "Institute for Policy Studies" performed the function for the Conspiracy of energizing and guiding the street revolutionaries in this country. He told how Arthur Waskow, one of the founders of the Institute, was predicting in 1971 that the "youth revolution" soon would be taking a surprising new twist, with the "youth" turning toward religion. As Gary Allen observed wryly, "It would be a mistake to rejoice over any 'religious revival' whose 'spiritual energies' had been brought together by the 'Institute for Policy Studies' from among its constituency of hippy and New Left elements." [10] Since 1971 we have seen hippy-type "religious" groups sprouting like toadstools around the country, causing untold distress among hundreds of respectable families whose children have been "converted" and sequestered in "religious" communes. This is another clear example of the Conspiracy's use of religion for its purposes. Although it is not directly related to the subject of this chapter, it is interesting that this blossoming of "youth religion" has coincided in time with the blossoming of the "rapture" cult.

Since the majority of the larger Protestant church congregations are "liberal", the Scofieldian doctrine is taught primarily in the smaller, independent congregations. Thus the spread of the doctrine has the superficial appearance today of being a spontaneous, grass-roots movement when in actuality it is just the opposite, having been promoted from the top down as we have seen in Chapter 7. The movement began in the four large cities of New York, Boston, Chicago, and St. Louis, and was spread from those cities to the northeastern and middle-western parts of the country. It was not until much later that the doctrine spread significantly to the Far West and the South, where it is today perhaps stronger than anywhere else. But, as late as 1944, a committee of the General Assembly of the Southern Presbyterian Church reported that the doctrine was incompatible with that church's Confession of Faith.[11] To a discerning observer, of course, the very fact that the doctrine is promoted by the Insider-controlled communications media is evidence enough that this is far from being a spontaneous, grass-roots movement, any more so than is the "religious youth" movement instigated by the "Institute for Policy Studies."

Sometimes the Scofieldians use Americanist literature, presenting it as supporting evidence that the "rapture" is near. Needless to say. when Americanist literature is so used, the reader is not motivated to do anything about the problems presented except to await the "rapture" and perhaps to take some "guns and groceries" precautions, in case the "rapture" should be delayed. An example of this use is the book "Amazing Prophecies of the 70's-It's Super K!" by Doug Clark, [12] in which Chapter 5 is a verbatim reprint of an article from "American Opinion" of June, 1975 entitled "Henry Kissinger-This Man Is On the Other Side." Clark's thesis, published in 1975, is that Henry Kissinger may be the Antichrist. We do not know whether Clark has since issued a revision or whether he is still staying with Henry, Gary Allen's excellent book "None Dare Call It Conspiracy" has been used in similar manner by at least one television preacher.

Such use of Americanist literature points out another aspect of the problem. A person who is aware of the Conspiracy and its many evil manifestations is much more susceptible to the doctrines of the "rapture" cult than is one who is unaware of the facts of present-day life. The average American, obsessed with improving his golf score and hypnotized by the toob, is less likely to believe in the imminence of a "tribulation" than is the Americanist who knows the score and has been putting his all into the battle but who, becoming weary or discouraged, embraces the "rapture" idea as a welcome relief from his responsibilities. The "rapture" cult could not operate more perfectly to neutralize patriots if it had been engineered to do exactly that.

Responsible pre-millenialists view the activities and attitudes described in this chapter, as well as those engaged in by Joe Goodbuddy, as perversions of their faith. They point out that those who claim to be able to perceive, from the "signs of the times", that these are or are not the very last days, are behaving in an unscriptural manner, contrary to Christ's declaration, "But of that day and that hour knoweth no man, no, not the angels which are in heaven, neither the Son, but the Father. Take ye heed, watch and pray: for ye know not when the time is." [13] They point out that, just as there have been perversions of Christianity almost from the beginning, so also there have been perversions of the pre-tribulation "rapture" doctrine, perhaps almost from the beginning.

The author recognizes that the history given in this and the preceding chapters may not be enough evidence to prove Conspiracy involvement in the phenomenal growth and perversion of the pretribulation "rapture" doctrine. Unfortunately, this is the usual situation when one delves into the more hidden recesses of the Conspiracy. Perhaps, though, it would be useful to assemble and observe at one time some of the more interesting bits and pieces of circumstantial evidence. The following are some this author has been able to discern:

(a) The sudden appearance in the British Isles, around the year 1830, of two dynamic religious leaders, Irving and Darby, both of whom were able to influence large numbers of people to leave their established churches to form new sects. Both sects promoted the same new, previously unknown, religious doctrine.

(b) The secrecy practiced in Irving's church, where it was forbidden for the "prophetic utterances" to be written down, or even to be repeated verbatim.

(c) Darby's unusual mobility, for his day and time, and his seeming lack of financial problems.

(d) The timing of Darby's work in America-at the same time that the "higher criticism" movement was taking root.

(e) The rather remarkable promotion of ex-Confederate C. I. Scofield, at the very young age of 30, to a responsible federal position. This was done by a Grant Administration which many students believe was heavily influenced by the contemporary Insiders of the Master Conspiracy.

(f) The assertion by Gaebelein that, as late as 1879, no theological seminary in America taught the type of theology which Dr. Brookes taught to Scofield, and which later appeared in Scofield's Bible.

(g) Scofield's unusual mobility, for his day and time, especially during the time of writing the Reference Bible; also, his seeming lack of financial problems, and his seemingly excellent contacts and connections in Europe.

(h) Publication of the Scofield Bible by the Oxford University Press. Informed patriots know the important part played by Oxford University in the promotion and spreading of Fabian Socialism in both England and America. [14] The fact that a university so saturated with the ideology of Godless collectivism should have published, and should continue to publish even today, a Bible which purports to uphold fundamental Christianity, should provide any Americanist with food for thought.

Scofield, who apparently had never before published anything except one small book and some pamphlets and tracts, seemed to have amazingly easy entree into one of the most prestigious and exclusive publishing houses in the English-speaking world.

(i) The timing of the appearance of the Scofield Bible, in the same decade in which the Conspiracy launched its open attack upon the large Protestant denominations, through the formation of the Federal Council of Churches and by other actions.

(j) The almost simultaneous origin and development of the British Israel and the Darbyite doctrines, and the similar manner in which both were disseminated beyond the sects in which they have their roots.

(k) Gaebelein's use of the "Protocols" as an authority in his book.

(l) The widespread promotion today of the pre-tribulation "rapture" doctrine through the establishment-controlled communications media, but with very little accompanying promotion of the main Christian message of salvation.

(m) The fruits of the theory-neutralization of active or potential opposition to the Conspiracy.

Any one of the above taken alone might be of little significance, and each could be attributed to normal influences or to coincidence. But taken together they do indicate a pattern, or at least the possibility of one. Certainly there is no proof that any one of the individuals mentioned was in any way directly involved with the Conspiracy, and it is possible that none was. But, to paraphrase an expression used many times regarding circumstances obviously benefiting the Conspiracy, if there had been no pre-tribulation "rapture" doctrine. the Conspiracy would have had to invent one. It may be that the Conspiracy had the incredibly good fortune that it all developed spontaneously. Or it may have originated spontaneously, subsequently receiving a nudge here and a pat on the back there, as needed, from the Conspiracy. Or it may have originated spontaneously and then was taken over and perverted at some point by the Conspiracy. Whatever the mechanism, it is certain that the vast majority of the people involved were innocent of any conspiratorial purpose, just as in most projects of the Conspiracy. But the tragic fact remains that the doctrine is having a devastating effect today in neutralizing current and potential opposition to the Master Conspiracy which seeks to enslave the world.

Possibly it is no coincidence that there is yet another neutralizing religious doctrine, which is held by many who do not accept the Scofieldian doctrine. This is the belief that a Christian must take absolutely no part in government or politics, even to the extent of abstaining from voting. Needless to say, those who believe in this doctrine are just as effectively neutralized from opposing the Conspiracy as are those who have folded their hands to await the "rapture." Since the Conspiracy seems to try to have something to mislead nearly everyone, it would be somewhat surprising to find that they were uninvolved in this particular belief, which serves their purposes so admirably. As chance would have it, this belief is a vital part of the doctrine of British Israel, as documented in the book, "The Plain Truth About Armstrongism."[15] The belief is not confined to British Israel by 15 any means, but is found in many other religious bodies as well. One of the leading sources of this belief is a book by David Lipscomb entitled "Civil Government." [16] *

 *The best refutations of Lipscomb's debilitating thesis are "The Sermon on the Mount and the Civil State [17] and "The Christian and the Government" [18], both by Foy E. Wallace, Jr.

In the Bulletin of The John Birch Society for April, 1972, Mr. Robert Welch had this to say: "The Communists have always proceeded on the age-old theory that the most important accomplishment in all forms of warfare is to paralyze your enemy's will to resist before coming to actual hostilities. There is no surer nor more deadly form of paralysis to inflict on their enemies than religious neutralism... (Devout Christians who have been neutralized) are the very people who should be most faithful and determined in their resistance to Communism. Instead they have been almost completely neutralized by a now gigantic scheme which the

Communists themselves have been skillfully promoting for over a hundred years. And if you do not believe that this whole development has been a most important part of the deliberate strategy of the Communists, then you had better go back and study the Conspiracy some more... The Communists have a tremendous facility for converting each of their worst liabilities into one of their greatest assets. The Communists, as deadly enemies of all religion, by infiltrating either false leadership or destructive doctrine into sacred places, have done a typically brilliant job of making the most religious people serve evil purposes, and contribute mightily to the intended suffocation of religion itself." [19] Although Mr. Welch was speaking of religious neutralism generally, and not of any particular doctrine specifically, Americanists would do well to consider seriously and carefully the principles he outlined.

In a highly informative book about the Conspiracy entitled "Karl Marx, Capitalist", June Grem observed in 1972 concerning religious neutralism: "Although much of the Bible has been challenged by agnostics and antagonists, it is of more than passing significance that this one issue should be singled out for unswerving acceptance. Christ said His Kingdom was not of this world but the political manipulators who are promoting world government use every method imaginable to con people into accepting the idea of global dictatorship. They will even attempt to make it look like Bible prophecy, if possible." [20]

But some devout, sincere Christians may object, "But I believe the Bible as the inspired Word of God. Does not the Bible teach these things?" Let us examine a quotation from MacPherson's excellent book, in which he quotes a personal letter he received: "An Oregon Bible teacher wrote: 'You will be interested to know that many years ago I had dinner in Seattle with a then middle-aged couple who were members of the Catholic Apostolic Church (Irvingite sect). At that time I believed in pre-tribism and told them so. They asked me where I got the doctrine. I told them "from the Bible." They said, "No, you didn't" and went on to tell me how it was not in the Bible but revealed to their church through one of their prophetesses around the middle of the 19th century." [21]

Does the Bible itself offer a more plausible alternative to the Scofieldian doctrine?

CHAPTER 9

THE THIRD SIDE OF THE QUESTION

"Seal not the sayings of the prophecy of this book: for the time is at hand."
Revelation 22:10 (Circa A.D. 68)

As we pointed out in Chapter 5, the two attitudes regarding the Bible which seem today to be pervasive throughout American culture are: (a) the Bible is filled with errors, myths and contradictions, and is not to be taken seriously by any intelligent, "modern" person; and (b) the Bible is the inspired Word of God, which teaches clearly that the Second Coming of Christ is imminent. The "tone setters" have done their work so well in establishing these two views as the "two sides" of the question that they have been able to obscure almost completely from the casual inquirer the fact that millions of devoted Christians in America and throughout the world hold to a third, entirely different, view. This view is that the Bible is the inspired Word of God, which teaches that no-one except God Himself knows when the Second Coming of Christ is to occur. Stated very broadly, this view probably would encompass the beliefs of most of the postmillenialists, a-millenialists and post-tribulation pre-millenialists who reject the "higher criticism" philosophy. It might well be called the "conservative" Protestant view, since it encompasses the entire range of Protestant beliefs held prior to about 1830. The beliefs expressed in the remainder of this chapter are not presented as the only possible doctrine which a reasonable and faithful person could hold, but are given as one example of an alternative to the Scofieldian doctrine.

While many passages in many different books of the Bible are interpreted in the Scofield Bible to support the Scofieldian thesis, the

Book of Revelation is central to his theory. It is the contention of Scofield and his followers that the Book of Revelation is a prophecy as yet unfulfilled, one which depicts catastrophic events soon to occur in our own time. An alternative view is that the Book of Revelation is a message conveyed by the Apostle John to warn the Christians of his own day of catastrophic events which were then imminent, and which did indeed occur. In this view, the Book of Revelation is a prophecy which has been fulfilled, just as many other Biblical prophecies have been fulfilled. Let us examine the book itself.

One of the first characteristics of the Book met by the reader is its sense of urgency. The very first verse of the first chapter reads: "The Revelation of Jesus Christ, which God gave unto him, to show unto his servants things which must shortly come to pass." Again, in the third verse, we read: "Blessed is he that readeth, and they that hear the words of this prophecy, and keep those things which are written therein: for the time is at hand." In the very last chapter, in verse 6, we read: "and the Lord God of the holy prophets sent his angel to show his servants the things which must shortly be done." The whole tone of the book is one of urgency. This would be entirely natural if John were speaking of things soon to occur in the first century, but hardly appropriate if he were speaking of events to occur nineteen hundred years in the future.

The second striking feature of the Book of Revelation is its use of symbolic language. Symbols are used profusely throughout the book, but for what purpose? If the book were a prophecy of events to occur in far distant centuries, why clothe them in symbols such as horsemen, locusts, beasts, etc.? Any answer to this question must be, at best, highly speculative. But, if the book were describing the Roman emperor and his government, and events which they would soon bring about, then the Apostle had every reason to clothe his warnings in symbolic language or, as we would term it today, in code. If he had given his warnings in plain language, he would have precipitated upon the Christians the immediate wrath of the empire, and the church might have been

64

completely obliterated. But by writing in code he could conceal his message from the Roman authorities while revealing it to the churches, since there were in every church in the first century those who were spiritually gifted. This is discussed by Paul at length in his first letter to the Corinthians. [1] For example, in First Corinthians 12:8, Paul says, "For to one is given by the Spirit the word of wisdom; to another the word of knowledge by the same Spirit." In Revelation 13:18, John says, "Here is wisdom. Let him that hath understanding count the number of the beast: for it is the number of a man; and his number is six hundred threescore and six." John knew that those who were spiritually gifted with wisdom would be enabled to decipher his cryptogram, in this case one giving the identity of the beast.

The identity of the beast is another clue to the nature of the Book of Revelation. The code number, 666, fits perfectly the official name of the emperor who was then on the throne of the Roman Empire, Nero Caesar. The numerical values of the letters making up his name in the Hebrew language add up to the infamous 666. What could have been more natural than for the Apostle to conceal his message from the Romans while revealing it to the Christians by employing the Hebrew language, unfamiliar to the Romans but familiar to many Christians? In searching for an answer to the ancient and mysterious 666, why overlook the most obvious answer? Nero, who reigned from A.D. 54 to A.D. 68, was the first emperor to persecute the Christians. Some scholars may object that Nero could not have been the beast because the Book of Revelation was written after his lifetime, in about A.D. 96. But this date is based upon flimsy evidence, and the preponderance of scholars place the date of the book during the period of Nero's reign, prior to the destruction of Jerusalem in A.D. 70. It is beyond the of this book to discuss this question, but the reader scope is referred to "The History of the Christian Church", in which the author, Phillip Schaff, the translator of the American Standard Version of the Bible, cites a list of twenty scholars who all agree upon the early date for the book.

If we are to conclude that the book of Revelation was indeed written as an urgent coded warning to the Christians of the first century. what then was the message? It warned of two things. One was the impending destruction of the City of Jerusalem and the Jewish theocratic state; the other was the impending persecution of Christians by the Roman Empire.

The destruction of Jerusalem is portrayed most vividly in Chapters 17 and 18, where the city is characterized as a harlot for having rejected the teachings of God. The destruction of Jerusalem was indeed a cataclysmic event. More than one million [2] people perished after a protracted siege in which the wretched inhabitants were reduced to eating the bodies of their own children. It was truly a time of "great tribulation, such as was not since the beginning of the world to this time, no nor ever shall be," [3] just as Christ Himself had foretold in Matthew 24, Mark 13, and Luke 21. In those passages Christ had warned those Christians who would be present in Jerusalem at the time of the great siege to flee the city in great haste, not taking time even to gather up their belongings. Thus the Book of Revelation is seen as a reiteration and extension, probably sometime in the decade of A. D. 60-70, of warnings given by Christ Himself in about A. D. 33. Christ had enumerated the signs of the impending catastrophe while He was yet on earth. Through John, He warned the Christians again when the event was nearly upon them.

The Christians heeded the warning. The historian Eusebius, the Bishop of Cesarea in Palestine, wrote in A. D. 324 that the Christians in Jerusalem fled and took refuge in the mountain country of Pella, beyond the Jordan River.[4] Thus Christ's admonition to flee to the mountains was directed to the Christians of the first century, not to American Christian patriots of the twentieth century, some of whom have succumbed to the "guns and groceries" neutralizing syndrome because of this misunderstanding. Eusebius goes on to explain, in the same passage, how the siege and destruction of Jerusalem in A.D. 70 were a fulfillment of the prophecy of Daniel, referred to by Christ in both Matthew 24 and Mark 13: "... when finally, the abomination of desolation, according to the prophetic declaration, stood in the very temple of God, so celebrated of old, but which now was approaching its total downfall and final destruction by fire." A few pages later, Eusebius reiterates that these cataclysmic events were indeed those prophesied by Christ. "All this occurred in this manner, in the second year of the reign of Vespasian, according to the predictions of our Lord and Saviour Jesus Christ, who by his divine power foresaw all these things as if already present at the time, who wept and mourned indeed, at the prospect, as the holy evangelists show in their writings." [5]

Warnings concerning impending persecutions of Christians are given in numerous places in the Book of Revelation, but are coupled with assurances that the faithful Christians who would suffer torture and death would receive their rewards in heaven. Thus, in Chapter 6, we read: "I saw under the altar the souls of them that were slain for the word of God, and for the testimony which they held: And they cried with a loud voice, saying, How long, O Lord, holy and true, dost thou not judge and avenge our blood on them that dwell on the earth? And white robes were given unto every one of them; and it was said unto them, that they should rest yet for a little season, until their fellow-servants also and their brethren, that should be killed as they were, should be fulfilled." [6] Then in Chapter 20 we read: "And I saw thrones, and they sat upon them, and judgment was given unto them: and I saw the souls of them that were beheaded for the witness of Jesus, and for the word of God, and which had not worshipped the beast, neither his image, neither had received his mark upon their foreheads, or in their hands; and they lived and reigned with Christ a thousand years." [7] The souls of the martyrs of Chapter 6, who were murdered by the Romans, were shown receiving their reward in Chapter 20, reigning in heaven with Christ. Nowhere else in the entire Bible except in Chapter 20 of Revelation is there any mention of a thousand-year reign. Those who believe that Christ will establish a political reign upon the earth for a thousand years (the "millenium") believe that the passage quoted above describes a scene on earth rather than one in heaven. The fact that John said he saw the "souls" reigning with Christ seems to this author conclusive evidence that the scene described is heavenly, not earthly.

It is neither within the scope of this chapter nor within the ability of the author to give a comprehensive survey of the body of religious thought which has been touched upon here. It is our hope, however, that we have been able to indicate to the reader that a body of thought does exist which holds the Word of God in reverence and which is of completely contrary to the Scofield doctrine. It is a body of thought which sees the Bible as a comprehensive whole whose parts are all complementary to one another. Although the Bible is made up many books written by many different human authors over a period of many centuries, it is welded together into one harmonious entity by the action of the Holy Spirit who guided each writer.

One example of this harmony exists in the portions of Matthew, Mark, and Luke referred to earlier. Here we have three writers describing the same event, each in his own words. When all three descriptions are seen as a warning by Christ of the coming destruction of Jerusalem, harmony exists among the three Gospels. But Scofield does not see it thus. Scofield and his followers maintain that, while Christ's discourse as recorded by Luke refers to the destruction of Jerusalem in A.D. 70, the same discourse, as recorded by Matthew and Mark, refers to a still future siege of Jerusalem which is to occur during the coming "tribulation." The reader is urged to read these three chapters for himself (Matthew 24, Mark 13, and Luke 21) and determine for himself which is the more harmonious, logical, straightforward, and reverent interpretation.

We have not discussed other books of the Bible, such as Daniel, which are used by the Scofieldians to support their theory. It must suffice here to say that in these cases the simpler, more straightforward interpretation is, in the author's opinion, the one which sees these Old Testament prophecies as having been fulfilled in the first coming of Christ and the establishment of His church. In contrast, the Scofieldian doctrine sees these prophecies as still unfulfilled, but about to be fulfilled in the very near future.

It is the contention of the Scofieldians that the establishment and "flowering" of the Nation of Israel is a fulfillment of prophecy in itself, and that it points to the imminence of further prophetic fulfillments. For one example among many, an article in "Faith Aflame", a magazine promoting the Scofieldian doctrine, states: "The Jewish nation is by far the greatest evidence of the imminent return of the Lord." [8] Let us examine how the Nation of Israel came into being.

CHAPTER 10

THE NATION OF ISRAEL

"Zionism is the most stupendous fallacy in Jewish history"
Henry Morgenthau, Sr.[1]
(Not to be confused with Henry Morgenthau, Jr., a probable member or
agent of the Conspiracy.)

To learn the background behind the modern Nation of Israel we need
again to go back in history, this time to the year 1881 and the city of St.
Petersburg in Czarist Russia. There, in March, the movement to establish
the Nation of Israel received its energizing impetus from the explosion
of a bomb. The bomb, thrown by a Russian revolutionary, murdered the
benign Czar Alexander II, ending his policy of conciliation toward the
Jews of Russia and inaugurating an oppressive reign under Czar
Alexander III.

Within months after the assassination, the Russian minister of the
interior, Count Nicolai Ignatiev, announced that, since the tolerant
policies of Alexander II had failed, harsh measures against Russian
Jewry were now in order. [2] The notorious pogroms, anti-Jewish riots
under thinly-veiled government sponsorship, soon followed, with the
loss of many Jewish lives and the extensive destruction of Jewish
property. Next came a series of anti-Jewish decrees, termed "temporary
regulations", which came to be known as the "May Laws" since they
were placed into effect on May 3, 1882. These "temporary" laws were so
repressive and restrictive on Jewish life that, by the year 1900, nearly
40% of Russia's Jews were dependent upon charity. [3] The combined
effect of the pogroms and the May Laws drove the Jews of Russia, in
desperation, to seek relief in whatever direction it could be found. As
chance would have it, leadership was available to the Russian Jews in
either of two directions.

One direction was into the underground revolutionary movement, and a minority of Jews did indeed become revolutionaries, participating in the subversive movement which culminated in the successful Communist subversion of Kerensky's government in late 1917, and in the consolidation of Communist control by 1922. Although the presence of many Jews in leadership positions in the Communist revolution has led some observers to the mistaken conclusion that Communism is a Jewish conspiracy, those Jews were in fact driven toward and led into an already-existing conspiracy by the events of 1881 and 1882. As all students of the Master Conspiracy are well aware, the Conspiracy by then was at least a hundred years old, fully capable of having planned and perpetrated those events. Certainly the Conspiracy benefited immensely from the entry into the revolutionary movement of so many Jews.

The second direction in which the hard-pressed Jews of Russia were encouraged to seek relief was emigration from the country. The idea of Zionism, the return of Jews to their original homeland of Palestine, had been discussed academically among a few Jewish leaders for many years, but very little of a practical nature had been accomplished. One of the first to promote the Zionist idea was Zvi Hirsch Kalischer, in writings published during the period 1843 to 1862, but most of the religious Jews of his time considered his proposals to be blasphemous. [4] Another promoter of the idea was Moses Hess, who in 1862 published "Rome and Jerusalem." Hess, a friend of Karl Marx when they were both students at the University of Bonn, [5] was a collaborator with both Marx and Engels, [6] a dedicated socialist, and a member of the First International. [7] Walter Laqueur in his "A History of Zionism" remarks at the "curious coincidence" that, in the same year of 1862 in which Hess's book "Rome and Jerusalem" appeared in western Germany, pamphlet on the same subject should appear in the Hebrew language in eastern Germany, written by Kalischer. Laqueur considers it "remarkable" that the two publications, emanating from two such diverse sources as a radical socialist and an ostensibly Orthodox rabbi, should appear at the same time advocating such similar doctrines and political solutions. [8] Laqueur follows the usual pattern of not daring or not wishing to call it conspiracy.

But in the 1860's and 1870's Zionism was an idea whose time had not yet come. It was advocated only by a tiny minority of Jews, discussed and debated by a few, denounced by a substantial number, and ignored by most. Since the Jews residing in the various European countries were experiencing better treatment during the nineteenth century than they had been accustomed to in previous centuries, they had no particular incentive for emigrating. But the assassination of Czar Alexander II and the tragic events which followed changed all this abruptly so far as the Russian Jews were concerned, and it was the Russian Jews who provided the main driving force toward Zionism. The Zionists among the Russian Jews were encouraged in their endeavors by Ignatiev, the minister of the interior, who advocated that the Jews should emigrate to Palestine instead of to America because, he maintained, in Palestine they would be able to preserve their national identity, which they would not be able to do in America. [9] *This solicitous preserver of the Jews' identity was the same minister of the interior who had instigated the pogroms and May Laws which provided the impetus in the first place for the Jews to emigrate. It is interesting to remember also that Ignatiev's pretext for initiating his repressive measures against the Jews was provided by bomb-throwing revolutionaries. Astute believers in the "conspiracy theory of history" will have little difficulty in recognizing here the classic tactic of pressure from below combined with pressure from above to achieve a conspiratorial objective.

*Although this chapter is concerned primarily with the Zionist aspect of Jewish emigration, the great mass of emigrants during this period came to the United States. Between 1881 and 1914, almost two million Jewish immigrants, mostly from Russia and Russian-controlled Poland and Lithuania, arrived in the United States. Three quarters of these settled on the lower east side of New York City,[12] and there were among them, *inevitably, a sprinkling of Communist revolutionaries. On March 27, 1917, two hundred seventy-five of these, led by Trotsky, boarded the S.S. Christiana in New York to return to Russia where they accomplished, with Lenin and his followers, the Communist takeover of Russia.* [13]

Although a trickle of Jews had been migrating to Palestine in the early decades of the nineteen centuries, migration could be said to have begun in earnest only in 1882. It was also in 1882 that Baron Edmond de Rothschild, of the French branch of this prominent family of the Conspiracy, began financial support of the Jewish colonies in Palestine. Between 1884 and 1900 he spent six million dollars on the Zionist colonies, which became his major philanthropic interest.[10] Between 1882 and 1903, 25.000 Jews migrated to Palestine. [11]

In 1897 the Zionists became formally organized on an international basis when they gathered at the First Zionist Congress in Basel, Switzerland. This and succeeding Congresses had as their main objective what became known as "political Zionism", the negotiating with the Turkish government, which then controlled Palestine, of a charter for a land settlement company which could undertake largescale Zionist settlements. These efforts failed, however, and no further significant progress was made by the movement until 1917. Failure of the Zionists to make more headway during these years was due firstly to the fact that most Jews had never heard of Zionism, and secondly to the fact that, among those who had, most were strongly opposed to the whole idea in all countries except Russia. Even in Russia, the Orthodox Jews were suspicious of it. [14]

The breakthrough which placed the Zionist movement on the sure road to success was the publishing by the British government of the Balfour Declaration in November, 1917. This document placed the British government on record as favoring the establishment of a national home for the Jews in Palestine, and pledging the support of the British government in bringing it about. Ostensibly, the key Zionist in maneuvering the British government into this commitment was a Russian-born Jewish chemist named Chaim Weizmann.

Chaim Weizmann was born and reared near Pinsk, which became in the late nineteenth century one of the hotbeds of Zionist ferment in Russia. [15] After completing his education as a chemist in Germany and Switzerland, where he became one of the younger leaders of the Zionist movement, he transferred his activities in 1904, at age 30, to England where he settled in Manchester. When Weizmann arrived in Manchester as an obscure chemist he knew very little English, had no job, and had only one acquaintance in the city, a fellow Zionist; but he did have some letters of introduction. [16] In less than two years he had obtained an audience with Prime Minister Arthur James Balfour to plead the Zionist cause." In succeeding years Weizmann became quite friendly not only with Lord Balfour [18] but also with Lloyd George, Chancellor of the Exchequer and later Prime Minister,[19] with Lord Robert Cecil, Assistant Secretary for Foreign Affairs, [20] with Albert Einstein, and with Baron Edmond de Rothschild. [22] Either Weizmann, [21] the thirty-year-old chemist, was the genius of the century, or his letters of introduction were potent indeed.

One of those who helped arrange high-level introductions for Weizmann was C. P. Scott, editor of the extreme left-wing newspaper, the Manchester "Guardian." Weizmann says he happened to meet Scott at a party. [23] Scott was one of the leading "liberals" in Manchester, which at that time was one of the leading left-wing centers of the British Isles. [24] Weizmann relates how, when he and Scott would meet in London, Scott's customary greeting was, "Now, Dr. Weizmann, tell me what you want me to do for you." [25]

The talented Dr. Weizmann, in addition to his 24-carat contacts and acquaintances, also was gifted with extraordinary foresight. He relates how in 1914, shortly after the start of World War I, he dropped in on Baron Rothschild on his way through Paris and was "astonished" to find that he and the Baron were agreed that (a) the war would spread to the Middle East (as it did), and (b) the Allies would win the war. [26] In 1916 Weizmann, by then a naturalized English citizen, arranged to buy some real estate in Palestine at a time when that country was in the hands of England's enemy, Turkey. Weizmann relates how Lady Grey Hill, from whom his group bought the property, was convinced by Weizmann's action that England was going to win the war, [27] Perhaps she knew something of Weizmann's connections, for in 1916 such a purchase would have entailed considerable risk for any ordinary British citizen. In 1916 the deciding factor in determining the outcome of the war, the entry of the United States on the side of the Allies, had not yet occurred. In fact, Woodrow Wilson was that year campaigning for re-election on the slogan "He kept us out of war." Did Weizmann have an exceptionally clear crystal ball, or did he have Insider information?

As negotiations toward the Balfour Declaration proceeded, it became clear to Weizmann that the main opposition to such a declaration was coming from the Jewish community of England. [28] The Orthodox Jews regarded Zionism as their mortal enemy. To quote Laqueur's "History of Zionism," it "was interpreted as the most recent and the most dangerous phase in the continuing Satanic conspiracy against the House of Israel." [29] So intense was this opposition from their own Jewish constituencies that the leading British politicians were hesitant about going through with the declaration, even though most of them had been "won over" by Dr. Weizmann. The factor which broke the deadlock and led directly to the declaration was a telegram to the British government from Col. E. Mandel House, acting for President Wilson, declaring the support of the American government for the declaration. [30] The telegram arrived at the strategic moment even though, only shortly before, President Wilson had considered such a declaration premature since the United States was not at war with Turkey, of which Palestine was a part. [31]

The Balfour Declaration was addressed to Lord Nathaniel Rothschild, the head of the English branch of the family at the time, and was named after Lord Balfour because he was then the British Foreign Minister and had long been one of the prime movers in promoting the declaration. Balfour's credentials are extremely interesting. Professor Carroll Quigley, an admirer and supporter of the Insiders, tells in his monumental "Tragedy and Hope" how a secret society was formed in 1891 by Cecil Rhodes, a close associate of the Rothschilds, with Arthur (Lord) Balfour proposed as a member of the "Circle of Initiates." [32] This secret society set up so-called Round Table organizations as front groups [33] a in England and the United States, and the Round Table groups in turn established fronts known as the Royal Institute of International Affairs (RIIA) in England and the Council on Foreign Relations (CFR) in the United States. [34] Thus, Lord Balfour was truly an Insider's Insider, two rings nearer the center of the Conspiracy than an ordinary member of the Council on Foreign Relations is today. Viewed in this context, Weizmann's amazing skill and/or good fortune in climbing the ladder of prestige after his arrival in England are better understood. Weizmann evidently had been selected by the British Insiders as their front man who would be able to "accomplish". by his "amazing powers of persuasion", what the Insiders had agreed among themselves beforehand would be done; namely, the establishment of a Jewish nation in Palestine. While Weizmann was no doubt an extremely capable man, his brilliance, like that of an electric light bulb, was due more to his connections than to anything generated by himself.

As we have mentioned, support for Zionism in the United States was of crucial importance in bringing the Balfour Declaration to a successful culmination. It should not surprise any knowledgeable reader to learn that the leader of Zionism in the United States during this period, Louis Brandeis, who was appointed to the Supreme Court in 1916 by Woodrow Wilson, was a man with deep conspiratorial connections. Brandeis's maternal grandfather and great grandfather were both members of the Frankists in Europe. [35] Brandeis's father, Adolph Brandeis, would have taken part in the 1848 Communist revolution in Bohemia but for the fact that he was stricken with typhoid fever at the time. [36] Finding it advisable to leave Bohemia in late 1848, after the revolution had failed, Adolph came to America where he traveled in the company of a friend of his family who was an agent of the Rothschilds. [37] Reared in America with this background, Louis Brandeis had become, by 1914, the Chairman of the Provisional Executive Committee for General Zionist Affairs. [38] As the official spokesman for American Zionists during the critical years of 1914-1917, Brandeis was in touch with President Wilson, James Rothschild, Louis de Rothschild. Secretary of State Lansing, the French Ambassador to Washington. Jusserand, and, of course, with Chaim Weizmann. He was assisted in his high-level promotion of the Zionist cause during these years by Rabbi Stephen Wise [39] who has been identified with at least thirty-three Communist front organizations. [40] When Lord Balfour visited Washington in May, 1917, Brandeis had luncheon with Balfour at the White House. Balfour told him, "You are one of the Americans I had wanted to meet." [41]

The rationale used to explain the Balfour Declaration to the British public was that it was a wartime political necessity, needed to consolidate Jewish world opinion on the side of the Allies. In actual fact. as we have seen already, Zionism was strongly, sometimes even violently, opposed by a majority of Jews everywhere except in Russia. But this fact was ignored by Allied propaganda in a typical reversal of the truth.

As the murder of Alexander II provided the initial impetus to Zionism, and as World War I provided the pretext for the crucial Balfour Declaration, so the persecution of the Jews in Germany by the Nazis, along with the turmoil following World War II, provided the needed impetus for mass Jewish migration to Palestine. These later events are too well known to require elaboration here except to note that the Nazis were brought into power by the Conspiracy, [42] and that both World Wars were engineered by the Conspiracy. [43] If these broad statements are too sweeping for the reader, the author makes no apology but refers the reader to the references cited. We do not mean to imply, of course, that both wars were instigated solely for the purpose of creating the Nation of Israel. The Conspiracy had many purposes and reaped many benefits from each of these wars, in addition to the one with which this chapter is concerned.

One specific occurrence related to World War II does need to be mentioned. At the end of the war, General Eisenhower conducted "Operation Keelhaul," in which thousands of "displaced persons" who had fled from eastern Europe were forcibly returned by Eisenhower's illegal orders to the Communist butchers from whom they had fled. [44] But, on direct orders from President Truman, those refugees who were Jewish were specifically ordered not to be returned, and in fact the flight of additional Jewish refugees from Poland was encouraged. [45] Thousand of these became emigrants to Palestine.

The final throes leading to the actual establishment of the independent Nation of Israel consisted of turmoil, violence, and terrorism involving the Jews, Arabs, and the British Army in Palestine. The chief features of this period were the assassination and terrorism inflicted by Jewish guerilla gangs against personnel of the British government and army. [46] These tactics were disavowed, of course, by the leading Zionists, but the ultimate result of this pressure, combined with continued heavy illegal immigration of the "displaced persons" from eastern Europe into Palestine, was to "force" the Socialist British government to give up and withdraw its troops. This strategy will ring all too familiar to present-day Americans, who can recall the use of a very similar strategy in the recent American withdrawal from Vietnam.

The final step in establishing the Nation of Israel was a vote in the United Nations, in late 1947, to partition Palestine into two parts, one of which was to be the new nation. [47] Informed Americanists need no references to document the domination of the United Nations by the Conspiracy, but for those who have not had the opportunity to learn of this we recommend G. Edward Griffin's "The Fearful Master." [48]

This chapter has been, at best, an extremely sketchy history of Zionism, but we hope to have shown informed Americanists that this history, at every crucial point, has been dominated by easily recognized strategies and tactics of the Conspiracy. Well known Conspiratorial names abound in the record, although only a few, such as the Rothschilds, Balfour, Louis Brandeis, and Col. House have been mentioned here. Other prominent names sprinkled through the annals are the Warburgs, Alfred Lord Milner, John Maynard Keynes, Leon Blum. Felix Frankfurter, and Henry Morgenthau, Jr. There can be little question that the Nation of Israel was planned and brought into being by the Conspiracy, to serve conspiratorial purposes.

Although American foreign policy has been ostensibly pro-Israel since the day of Israel's founding, it takes only a little reflection on recent history to discover that some of the most serious injuries inflicted upon that nation have been perpetrated by the United States government. In 1956, for example, Eisenhower forced a halt to the combined military operation of the Israelis, French, and British, which otherwise would have resulted in the defeat of Egypt and the liberation of the Suez Canal which Egypt had stolen. In 1973 Kissinger stopped the Israelis from annihilating the Egyptian Third Army, forcing the Israelis to allow the Egyptians to escape. It was Kissinger again who forced the Israelis to withdraw 22 miles inland from the Suez Canal, giving up an easily defended natural boundary for one not easily defended, at the same time giving Egypt uncontested control of the canal once more. It is the American government which today is pressuring Israel to deal with the Communist terrorist PLO as though they were a decent, civilized government. The truth is that the Insiders of the Conspiracy, working through their agents in the American, Russian, and Israeli governments, are manipulating the Nation of Israel like a puppet for the benefit of the Conspiracy.

Today the existence of the Nation of Israel serves a multitude of purposes for the Conspiracy, not the least of which is the one which prompted the writing of this chapter. For the existence of the Nation of Israel is used by the Scofieldians today as the key ingredient in convincing not only fundamental Christians, but many of the general public as well, that the "rapture" must be imminent and therefore any resistance to the Conspiracy is not only futile but unnecessary.

CHAPTER 11

PINNING THE TAIL ON THE BEAST

"Our enemies laugh among themselves." Psalm 80:6

One of the cardinal beliefs of the "rapture" cultists is that the Antichrist is about to make his appearance. Although they expect to be "raptured" before the Antichrist begins his evil reign (the "tribulation"), their belief that the "rapture" is imminent necessitates a belief also that the Antichrist is waiting in the wings, almost ready to reveal himself. Therefore, there has been continual speculation about the identity of the Antichrist.

Margaret Macdonald, on the same evening in 1830 when she first put forth her new pre-tribulation "rapture" idea, also mentioned that the Antichrist was Robert Owen (1771-1858).[1] Owen, one of the leading Insiders of his day, was indeed an evil man.* Many of his writings are included in "The Life and Ideas of Robert Owen",[3] published in recent years by International Publishers, the openly Communist publishing house in New York City. Present day Communists revere Owen as the father of modern Communism. He did not, however, make the grade as Antichrist.

In the opening address of the Campbell-Owen Debate held in Cincinnati, Ohio in April, 1829, Owen called for the abolition of marriage and the family, abolition of religion, abolition of private property and the establishment of an entire new order of things.[2]

MacPherson quotes Robert Baxter of Doncaster, England, who wrote in 1833: "The person who should be so energized of Satan, and be set up as his Christ, was at a subsequent period, declared to be young Napoleon."[5] This, of course, referred to Napoleon III (1808-1873), not to the famous general. Baxter was a former member of the Catholic Apostolic Church who, by 1833, had become "completely convinced that the Irvingite movement in London was not of God." [6]

During World War I many Christians thought they had identified the Kaiser as Antichrist. During World War II many were equally certain about Hitler. The most popular modern candidate for Antichrist, until just recently, was Henry Kissinger.[7] Now that Henry seems to have exited, or at least has left the center of the stage, it will be most interesting to learn who inherits his mantle as Antichrist Presumptive. Perhaps it may be Ralph Nader, who was suggested recently by one lady who should have been a prospect for Birch membership, but who was too pre-occupied with speculation about whether the beast would be a Jew or an Arab. She seemed to favor the latter, hence her interest in Nader, a Lebanese.*

*On an unsolicited cassette tape mailed from Macon, Georgia to numerous Birch Society leaders in the Southeast, the speaker confirms that he has identified the Genuine Beast a computer located in Belgium! Some cultists, in the past, have given definite dates for the fulfillment of various events in their prophetic scheme of things to come. During World War II, for example, the Rev. Frank Hamilton, [12] who believed some of the "tribulation" would occur before the "rapture", predicted "tribulations" extending from 1952 or '53 through the summer of 1955 or '56, forecast that the "rapture" would occur in the late fall or early winter of 1959 or 1960,[14] and saw the "millennium" beginning in the spring of 1963 or '64. [15] The Rev. Hamilton lists in his book the following colleges which at that time taught the Scofieldian doctrine: "This view is held by Faith Seminary; some teachers at Princeton Seminary; Wheaton College; Maryville College: Dallas Theological Seminary: Columbia Bible College; Davidson College; Wilson College; Beaver College; Asbury College; William Jennings Bryan College: Bob Jones College; Union Bible Seminary." [17]

Naming of Antichrists has not been confined, of course, to these cultists, since it was being done long before their time. Many of the early leaders of the Protestant Reformation believed that the Papacy was the Antichrist.[8] During the time of Napoleon Bonaparte, many thought Napoleon was the Antichrist.[9] There have been many other candidates throughout Christian history, as described by Foy E. Wallace, Jr. in his monumental "The Book of Revelation."[10] "There have been almost a legion of names in many different languages that have been deciphered in the efforts to find the solution for Code 666, ranging from the merest conjecture to a frantic religious fanaticism that borders on lunacy. The names of ancient political war lords, medieval papal pontiffs, together with nineteenth and twentieth century dictators, have been juggled to yield the sum 666." [11]

Modern-day seers are more wary about setting dates and frequently caution one another against doing so, although occasionally one will still yield to the temptation. One such is the Rev. Arnold Murray, who advises on one of his cassette tapes:[16] "If you understand Hebrew, in the fortieth chapter of Ezekiel it also says that this dispensation will come near an end somewhere around the year 1982." To observe an example of just how far some of these modern "prophets" will stretch the Bible, the reader is urged to read the fortieth chapter of Ezekiel and to try to ascertain where the Rev. Murray discerns this "prophecy." Evidently he did not expect any of his listeners to take the trouble to consult the Bible, but for any who might do so he included the proviso that they must "understand Hebrew."

If the Christians of the British Isles in the mid-nineteenth century, instead of cringing before Robert Owen, hoping for an imminent "rapture", had organized themselves into a movement to expose Owen and his evil associates, we might today live in a much better and saner world. Robert Owen was indeed a great influence for evil, and his exposure might have set back the Conspiracy immensely. Similarly, if those Christians who recognized Henry Kissinger for the evil influence he has been during the past few years had joined in the effort to expose him and his fellow conspirators, the Conspiracy would today be much less advanced than it is. Let us hope that, in the days ahead, a significant number of Christians may face up to their moral responsibilities on this earth, leaving the cosmic decisions to the Lord Almighty. Then, the Lord willing, the descendants of present-day Christians may be able to look upon their ancestors with gratitude and pride, rather than with chagrin and despair.

It should be emphasized that not everyone who uses the Scofield Bible, or who believes in similar doctrines, is neutralized in the struggle against evil. There are many Christian patriots who do hold this belief but who also feel they have a responsibility to uphold the civilization they inherited from their forefathers, a civilization which, imperfect though it may be, still is based upon Christian principles. These, perhaps, are as good a proof as we have of the truth of one of Robert Welch's favorite sayings, "Morality sees farther than intellect." To these, at least as much honor is due as to the patriot who looks upon the struggle as a matter of life or death, freedom or slavery, civilization or dark ages, in a future whose duration is to him not a matter for speculation. As much honor is due the former, that is, if he works with equal fervor and dedication. Unfortunately there are almost-neutralized Birchers who, as they began to believe that the Second Coming would soon solve all their earthly problems, reduced the intensity of their activity from "full speed ahead" to "I'll go through a few motions." It might be said that these have joined the "rapture chapter." Sadly, the motivation provided by a desire to do what is morally right is, with all too many of us, not a strong driving force. The weaknesses of human nature are ever with us in this struggle; we all have them and we all need to overcome them.

CHAPTER 12

HOW DO YOU STAND?

"It is Satan not God who has been urging you to become a coward in this raging battle between good and evil, and to leave what should be your duty all up to God." Robert Welch, 1972

Researching and writing this book has been rather like exploring a labyrinthine cave. Aware at the outset only of a yawning dark chasm called "religious neutralism," we entered with our flashlight. We have explored to a certain extent what appears to be the main passageway, bypassing in the process many side passages down which we could catch fleeting but tantalizing glimpses. All of these side passages and much of the main passage remain to be explored, but the urgency of the problem compels us at this point to emerge from the cave and publish what we have learned so far. There may be readers who know much more about the subject than we, and perhaps there may be other readers who will be motivated to delve into the subject on their own. The bibliography included in this book may serve as a useful starting point for any who have this interest. Certainly much more evidence needs to be amassed.

The writing and publishing of this book were not undertaken lightly, since the author is well aware that it may make him more enemies than friends. The author has many good friends whose religious beliefs may be offended by what has been said, some of them Americanists still engaged in the war. While they, to their credit, have not been neutralized, the author asks them to reflect for a moment on all the others with similar beliefs who have dropped out of the war. This book has been written not because the author wished to offend anyone, but because it had become painfully obvious that the job simply had to be done.

In 480 B.C. the Persian army, estimated to have numbered about three million, advanced down the coast of Greece from the north, threatening to conquer all of Greece and to destroy Greek civilization. The Greek leaders resolved to resist the Persian invasion at a narrow pass between the mountains and the ocean known as Thermopylae, but it was time for the annual Olympic Games, and the Greeks were torn between their desire to save their country and their desire to participate in the games. Taking what must have been one of the most foolish gambles in all human history, the Greek leaders dispatched a small force of about 7000 with orders to hold the pass for a week until the games could be completed and the main army could be sent to reinforce them. The small defense force, with extreme valor, did succeed in blocking the Persian advance for several days, and might have held out for the entire week had it not been for two other elements which entered the picture. First, a Greek traitor disclosed to the Persians a secret route over the mountains, bypassing the position of the defenders at Thermopylae. Then a force of Greeks assigned to guard this path deserted their posts, allowing the Persians to encircle the main defenders and attack from the rear. Although the Greeks rallied later and saved their country by their naval victory at Salamis, this was not accomplished until after Athens and other Greek cities had been laid waste by the invaders.[1]

In the tragedy of Thermopylae we can see several striking parallels with our situation today. We have "American" traitors working with the enemy to destroy our country. We have a vast majority of our population more interested in playing games than in defending their country. We have a small but valiant defense force, capable of turning the tide if given adequate support and loyalty. And we have former defenders who have deserted their posts.

When the Communists took control of China, there were among the Chinese who had been converted to Protestant Christianity two groups - those who believed in the imminent "rapture" and those who did not. Those who believed in the Scofieldian doctrine remained where they were, confident that they were to be rescued from danger at any moment by the "rapture." They were tortured and slaughtered by the tens of thousands. Those, on the other hand, who did not believe in the imminent "rapture" fled to the mountains where many have been able to survive, keeping at least a few embers of Christianity glowing, however faintly. [2] The Christians who fled did the only thing they were able to do to help preserve their heritage. They were unable to save their country through a John Birch Society or by any other means, since the fate of their country had been sealed by "American" traitors concealed in the American government. [3] But the Christians did what they could, with the means at their disposal.

We Americanists today face an awesome responsibility. While we, along with Americans in general, continue to enjoy the comforts and benefits inherited from long centuries of civilizing endeavors, it is only we Americanists who are aware of the extreme precariousness of our whole civilized structure. Plainly and simply, if America and Western Civilization are to be saved, the saving must be done by a relative handful of informed and dedicated Americanists. It can be done.

Few in number though we may be, we are orders of magnitude better equipped than were the Chinese Christians to combat the enemy. Where the Chinese were helpless against the military onslaught of the Communists, we face not bullets but rather lies, deceit, and treason. We are in a war the outcome of which will be determined by whether truth or falsehood prevails. We have the knowledge, the leadership, the organization, the money (although not yet made available in sufficient quantities), and the skills needed to win a war of this nature. The only necessary ingredient which today appears to be in questionable supply is the will to win.

The burning question today is, which group of Chinese Christians shall we Americanists emulate? Will it be those who did what they could with what they had, or will it be those who, paralyzed in will, did nothing but pray to be raptured? Shall we be remembered in history like those who, at the crucial moment in the Battle of Thermopylae, deserted their posts, or like those who fought bravely against overwhelming odds?

Being a Bircher has its rewards as well as its responsibilities. It puts the patriot into close contact with the finest body of people in the world today, people who know the score and have accepted their responsibilities. It enables the patriot to become and to remain better informed than he could possibly be on his own, giving him a continually increasing understanding of how all the pieces of the puzzle fit together. It gives one the overwhelming sense of satisfaction that comes from knowing one is doing his duty, while helping to make history. As one Bircher summed it up. "Happiness is being a Bircher!" In spite of contending strenuously in a deadly serious battle, Birchers are indeed among the happiest people alive. The only happier people are Christian Birchers.

If you are not a Bircher and have endured this far in this book, you need to become a Bircher. You can do so by contacting any member you may know, or by writing The John Birch Society. Belmont, Mass., 02178. If you're a former Bircher who may have succumbed to one of the neutralizers, why not re-instate your membership and get back to work? You will be welcomed back with open arms. We who are John Birchers or who ought to be John Birchers are a special breed of people. Why is it that we, unlike the vast majority, have been able to see through the smokescreen and discern the truth?

The answers are as varied as there are individuals, of course, but let us consider the possibility that, in one way or another. God has placed upon each of us a special burden of responsibility and is watching to see how each of us stands up under that burden. Some stand and some fall, as we pointed out at the beginning. The outcome of this war and the fate of our civilization will be determined, in all probability, by how many do stand, and how well.

"We shall meanly lose or nobly save the last hope of earth."
Abraham Lincoln

ABOUT THE AUTHOR

Robert L. Pierce has been a member of The John Birch Society since 1962, a Chapter Leader since 1963, and a volunteer Section Leader since 1964. He became a Christian in 1963 as a direct result of having first become a Bircher. A chemical engineer by profession, he makes his living in research and development work within the synthetic textile fibers industry.

RECOMMENDED READING AND REFERENCES

CHAPTER 1

RECOMMENDED READING LIST
"NONE DARE CALL IT CONSPIRACY," Gary Allen For Americans worried about the growing power of government, no better introduction to the persons and plans responsible for that growth has yet been published.

"THE NAKED CAPITALIST," W. Cleon Skousen This review of leftist Carroll Quigley's "Tragedy and Hope" presents an outstanding introduction to the Insiders' conspiracy to rule the world.

"THE TRUTH IN TIME," Robert Welch An overview of two hundred years of conspiracy, by the world's top authority on the subject.

"THE POLITICIAN," Robert Welch The fully documented story of Dwight David Eisenhower, in one of the most controversial books of the twentieth century.

"THE BLUE BOOK OF THE JOHN BIRCH SOCIETY," Robert Welch The transcript of the two-day presentation given at the founding meeting of the John Birch Society in Indianapolis, Indiana. December 8 and 9, 1958.

"PROOFS OF A CONSPIRACY," John Robison

"THE LAW," Frederick Bastiat

"JUDICIAL TYRANNY," Carroll Kilgore A comprehensive study of usurpation of state sovereignty by unconstitutional dictums of the federal judiciary.

REFERENCES
1. Robison, John, A.M., Professor of Natural Philosophy, and Secretary to the Royal Society of Edinburgh-"Proofs of a Conspiracy"-George Forman, No. 64 Water St., New York, N.Y., 1798. Re-published by Western Islands, Boston and Los Angeles, 1967.

2. Fitzpatrick, John C., Editor, "The Writings of George Washington from the Original Manuscript Sources, 1745-1799," prepared under direction of the Washington Bicentennial Commission-Printed June, 1941, U. S. Govt. Printing Office, Washington, D. C., Volume 36, pp. 452-453 and 518-519.

3. Anonymous "The John Franklin Letters," The Bookmailer, New York, 1959, See also pamphlet "What Can I Do To Combat Communism?" Christian AntiCommunism Crusade, Houston, Texas, 1960.

4. Hunter, Edward "The New Drive Against the Anti-Communist Program, "Testimony before the Senate Subcommittee on Internal Security, July 11, 1961.

5. Welch, Robert-The Neutralizers," The John Birch Society, Belmont, Mass. 02178, 1963.

CHAPTER 2

REFERENCES

1. Granovsky. Anatoli-"I Was An NKVD Agent," Devin-Adair, 23 E. 26th St., New York, 1962. Pocket edition by Western Islands, Belmont. Mass. 02178, 1967. See especially Chapter 17, pp. 173-176.

2. Stormer, John A., "None Dare Call It Treason," The Liberty Bell Press, P.O. Box 32, Florissant, Mo., 1964. (Probably out of print, but millions of copies exist.
See your nearest veteran Bircher.)

3. Gumaer, David Emerson, "Apostasy-The National Council of Churches," "American Opinion," Belmont. Mass. 02178, Feb. 1970, pp. 49-68.

4. Stormer, Op. Cit., pp. 125-126.

5. Pope Pius XI, "Quadragesimo Anno," May 15, 1931.

6. Pope Pius XI-"Divini Redemptoris"-1937.

7. Fenton, Fr. Francis, "Communism and America's Churches," "American Opinion," Belmont, Mass. 02178,

8. Antelman, Rabbi Marvin, "To Eliminate the Opiate," Zahavia, Ltd., 1 East 42nd St., New York 10018, 1974. The book referred to here is designated as Volume 1. Volume 2 is promised by Rabbi Antelman, and may now be available.) "

9. Ibid., p. 96.

10. Ibid., p. 142.

11. Ibid., pp. 17-32.

CHAPTER 5

REFERENCES5

1. Anonymous, Seventeen Eighty-Nine, An unfinished manuscript which explores the early history of The Communist Conspiracy, American Opinion, Belmont, Ma.. San Marino, Calif. 1968, p. 23.

2. Festinger, Leon et al., "When Prophecy Fails," Harper & Row. New York, 1964, pp. 12-33. See also Ref. 3 below.

3. Wallace, Foy E., Jr., "God's Prophetic Word." Foy E. Wallace, Jr. Publications, Oklahoma City, 1946, Revised Edition, 1960, pp. 231-232. Bennett, Arnold, "The Journal of Arnold Bennett, 1896-1928, "The Viking Press, New York, 1933, p. 743.

4. Chattanooga, "News-Free Press," May 3, 1976.

CHAPTER 6

REFERENCES

1. MacPherson, Dave "The Incredible Cover-Up", subtitled "The True Story On The Pre-Trib Rapture"-Logos International, Plainfield, N. J. 07061, 1975-Library of Congress Catalog Card Number 75-25171.

2. Norton, Robert, M. D."The Restoration of Apostles and Prophets: In the Catholic Apostolic Church"-1861-p. 15, as quoted by 2MacPherson (Ref. 1), p. 37.

3. MacPherson, Op Cit., p. 86.
4. Baxter, Robert, "Narrative of Facts, Characterizing the Supernatural Manifestations in Members of Mr. Irving's Congregation, and Other Individuals. In England and Scotland, and Formerly in the Writer Himself," Doncaster, England. 1833, p. 126, as quoted by MacPherson (Op. Cit.), p. 89.
5. Encyclopedia Britannica, Eleventh Edition, New York, 1910, Volume VIII. P. 600.
6. MacPherson, Op. Cit., p. 83.
7. Sandeen, Ernest R. "The Roots of Fundamentalism"-The University of Chicago Press, 1970, p. 38.
8. Ibid., p. 31.
9. MacPherson, Op. Cit., p. 32.

CHAPTER 7

REFERENCES
1. Sandeen, Ernest R."The Roots of Fundamentalism"-The University cago Press, 1970-p. 71.
2. Ibid., pp. 71 & 72.
3. Ibid., pp. 73 & 74.
4. Ibid., pp. 74 & 75.
5. Ibid., pp. 77 & 78.
6. Ibid., pp. 74 & 78.
7. "Our Hope", published by Gaebelein, and "Watchword and Truth", published by Cameron..
8. Sandeen, Op. Cit., p. 220.
9. Ibid., Chapter 10.
10. Orwell, George "Nineteen Eighty Four"-Harcourt, Brace & Co., New York, 1949.
11. Sandeen, Op. Cit., p. 236.
12. The Moody Monthly", Dec. 1933, p. 208, quoted by Spann (Ref. 13).

13. Spann, Robert L-The Achilles Heel of Conservatism", unpublished manuscript, Smithville, Tenn., 1973, p. 31.

14. Welch, Robert-"The Truth In Time"-"American Opinion" Magazine, Belmont, Mass. 02178, Nov., 1966, p. 10.

15. Sandeen, Op. Cit., pp. 214 & 215.

16. Ibid., p. 215.

17. Gaebelein, Arno Clemens-"Half a Century-The Autobiography of a Servant" Our Hope Publications, 456 Fourth Ave., New York, N.Y., 1930.

18. BeVier, William A.-"A Biographical Sketch of C. 1. Scofield"-A Thesis Presented to the Faculty of the Graduate School of Southern Methodist University in Partial Fulfillment of the Requirements for the Master of Arts with a Major in History-1960-pp. 10 & 11.

19. Ibid., p. 15.

20. Ibid., p. 15.

21. Ibid., p. 20.

22. Trumbull, Charles G., "The Life Story of C. I. Scofield," Oxford University Press, American Branch, 35 West 32nd Street, N.Y. 1920, p. 25.

23. Gaebelein, Arno C.-"The History of the Scofield Reference Bible"-Our Hope Publications, 456 Fourth Ave., New York, 1943-p.

24. BeVier. Op. Cit., p. 28.

25. Sandeen, Op. Cit., p. 191.

26. Gaebelein, Op. Cit., p. 37.

27. Ibid., p. 49.

28. Ibid., p. 49.

29. Ibid., p. 49.

30. BeVier, Op. Cit., pp. 72-81.

31. Gaebelein, Op. Cit., p. 62.

32. Sandeen, Op. Cit., p. 222. The Information on British Israel is excerpted from: (a) Toro, Carl-"British Israel"-unpublished manuscript-Downey, Calif. 90242 and (b) Welch, Robert, "The Neutralizers" The John Birch Society, Belmont, Mass. 02178, 1963.

CHAPTER 8

REFERENCES

1. Gaebelein, Arno Clemens, D.D. The Conflict of the Ages"-Published by Pryor N. Russell (no address given), 1966.

2. Ibid., pp. 99-103.

3. Welch, Robert-"The Neutralizers" The John Birch Society, Inc., Belmont, Mass. 02178, 1983-pp. 13-14.

4. Gaebelein, Op. Cit., p. 99. The passages cited are: Matthew 24:33; Mark 13:29: Luke 21:31: Revelation 1:3: Revelation 22:10; Daniel 12:4; 1 Thessalonians 5:4; and Matthew 24:13.

5. Bernstein, Herman-"The Truth About The Protocols of Zion"-CoviciFriede, New York, 1935.

6. Sandeen, Ernest R.-"The Roots Of Fundamentalism"-The University of
Chicago Press, 1970-p. 223.

7. The Merv Griffin Show, CBS Television, November, 1976. The author has a tape of this program.

8. Walvoord. John F. and Walvoord, John E.-"Armageddon-Oil and the Middle East Crisis" Zondervan Publishing House, Grand Rapids, Mich. 49506, 1974Library of Congress Catalog Card No. 74-4946.

9. MacPherson, Dave "The Incredible Cover-Up", subtitled "The True Story On The Pre-Trib Rapture"-Logos International, Plainfield, N. J. 07061, 1975-Library of Congress Catalog Card No. 75-25171.

10 Allen, Gary-"Making Plans for a Dictatorship in America"-"American Opinion" magazine, Belmont. Mass. 02178, April, 1971, p. 8.

11. Sandeen, Op. Cit., p. 265.

12. Clark, Doug "Amazing Prophecies of the 70's-It's Super K!"-Amazing Prophecy Center, Orange, Calif. 92667, 1975.

13. Mark 13:32, 33.

14. Martin, Rose L.-"Fabian Freeway"-Western Islands, Boston and Los Angeles, 1966.

15. Chambers, Roger R.-The Plain Truth About Armstrongism-Baker Book House, Grand Rapids, Mich., 1972, p. 11.

16. Lipscomb, David,"Civil Government," Gospel Advocate Co., Nashville, T., 1957, originally published 1866-67.

17. Wallace, Foy E., Jr.-"The Sermon on the Mount and the Civil State"-Foy E. Wallace, Jr., Publications, P.O. Box 7410, Ft. Worth, Texas 76111, 1967.

18 Wallace, Foy E., Jr. "The Christian and the Government"-Foy E. Wallace, Jr. Publications, P.O. Box 7410, Ft. Worth, Texas 76111, 1968.

19. Welch, Robert-"The Bulletin of the John Birch Society"-The John Birch Society, Inc., Belmont, Mass. 02178, April, 1972, pp. 13-14.

20. Grem, June "Karl Marx, Capitalist"-Enterprise Publications, Inc., P.O. Box 448, Oak Park, Ill. 60303, 1972, p. 22.

21. MacPherson, Op. Cit., p. 94. 1957 (Originally Published in 1866-67).

CHAPTER 9

REFERENCES

1. First Corinthians, Chapters 12, 13, and 14.

2. "The Ecclesiastical History of Eusebius Pamphilus, Bishop of Cesarea, in Palestine, Translated from the Original with an Introduction by Christian Frederick Cruse"-Baker Book House, Grand Rapids 6, Michigan, 1955, Book III, Chapter VII, p. 93.

3. Matthew 24:21.

4. Eusebius (Op. Cit.), Book III, Chapter V, p. 86.

5. Ibid., Book III, Chapter VII, p. 93.

6. Revelation 6:9-11.

7. Revelation 20:4.

8. Falwell, Jerry. Dr.-"How Near Is The End?"-"Faith Aflame" magazine, Lynchburg, Va. 24505-Nov.-Dec. 1976, p. 2.

CHAPTER 10

REFERENCES

1. Morgenthau, Henry, Sr.-"All In A Lifetime"-Doubleday, Page & Co., Garden City, NY, 1922.

2. Sachar, Howard M.-"A History of Israel"-Alfred A. Knopf. New York, 1978 - p. 12

3. lbid., p. 13.

4. Ausabel, Nathan-"Pictorial History of the Jewish People"-Crown Publishers, Inc., New York, 1953-p. 300.

5. Sachar, Op. Cit., p. 10.

6. Laqueur. Walter "A History of Zionism"-Holt, Rinehart and Winston, New York, Chicago, San Francisco, 1972-p. 46.

7. Ibid., p. 54.

8. Ibid., p. 54.

9. Ibid., p. 69.

10. Sachar, Op. Cit., p. 30.

11 Ibid., p. 26.

12. Ausabel, Op. Cit., pp. 282, 283.

13. Allen, Gary-"None Dare Call It Conspiracy"-Concord Press, Rossmoor,
Calif., 1971-pp. 68, 69.

14 Sachar, Op. Cit., p. 96.

15 Weizmann, Chaim-Trial and Error"-The Weizmann Foundation, 1949-
Schocken Books, Inc., New York, 1966-p. 24.

16. Ibid... p. 95.

17. Ibid., pp. 109-111.

18. Ibid., pp. 152-154.

19. Ibid., pp. 149-150, 157.

20. Ibid., p. 191.

21. Ibid., p. 118.

22 Ibid., p. 137.

23. Ibid., p. 149.

24. Ibid., pp. 119-120.

25. Ibid., p. 150.

26. Ibid., p. 148.

27. Ibid., p. 137.

28. Ibid., pp. 207-208.

29. Laqueur, Op. Cit., p. 407.

30. Ibid., p. 208.

31. Ibid., p. 208.

32. Quigley, Carroll-Tragedy and Hope"-The Macmillan Co., New York
p. 131.

33. Ibid., p. 132.

34 Ibid., p. 132.

35. Mason, Alpheus Thomas-"Brandeis-A Free Man's Life"-The Viking
New York, 1946, p. 441.

36. Ibid., p. 12.

37. Ibid., p. 15.

38. Ibid., p. 444.

39. Ibid., p. 452.

40 Gannon, Francis X. Biographical Dictionary of the Left, Vol. IV.,
Western Islands, Boston and Los Angeles, 1973, pp. 639-641.

41. Mason, Op. Cit., pp. 444-453, Beach, Calif. 90740, 1976.

42. Sutton, Antony C-"Wall Street and the Rise of Hitler"-76 Press, Seal

43. Welch, Robert "The Truth In Time"-"American Opinion" Magazine,
Belmont, Mass. 02178, November 1966, pp. 8-12, (See also the 85
documentary references included with this article.)

44. Welch, Robert-"The Politician"-Belmont Publishing Co., Belmont,
Mass. 02178, 1964 Chapter 4.

45. Sachar, Op. Cit., pp. 249-250.

46. Ibid., pp. 247-248, 264-267.

47. Ibid., pp. 292-295.

48. Griffin, G. Edward "The Fearful Master"-Western Islands, 395
Concord Ave., Belmont, Mass. 02178, 1964.

CHAPTER 11

REFERENCES

1. MacPherson, Dave "The Incredible Cover-Up" (see Ref. (1), Chapter 6)-pp. 156-157.

2. Campbell-Owen Debate on the Evidences of Christianity, McQuiddy Printing Co. Nashville, Tn. 1957, p. 3

3. Morton, A. L-The Life and Ideas of Robert Owen"-International Publishers, 381 Park Ave. South. New York, 1962 & 1969. The New 4. Encyclopedia of Social Reform, Third Edition-Funk and Wagnalls Co. New York and London, 1910, p. 859.

5. Baxter, Robert-"Narrative of Facts", etc., (see Reference (4). Chapter 8. as quoted by MacPherson, Op. Cit., p. 88.

6. MacPherson, Op. Cit., p. 89.

7. Clark, Doug "Amazing Prophecies of the 70's-It's Super KI" Amazing Prophecy Center, Orange, Calif. 92667, 1975.

8. MacPherson, Op. Cit., p. 25.

9. Ibid., p. 26

10. Wallace, Foy E., Jr.-"The Book of Revelation"-The Foy E. Wallace, Jr. Publications, P. O. Box 1301, Nashville, Tenn., 1966.

11. Ibid., p. 300.

12. Hamilton, Frank-"The Bible and the Millennium"-Rev. Frank Hamilton, 6701 Atlantic Ave., Ventnor, N. J-No date given, but the text indicates the book was written during World War II. .

13. Ibid., pp. 21-24

14. Ibid., p. 34.

15 Ibid., p. 42.

16. Murray, Arnold, Rev.-"Answers"-cassette tape-American Christian Congress, Gravette, Ark. 72736, Side 2 (Advertised in "The Spotlight")

17. Hamilton, Op. Cit., Preface, p. i.

CHAPTER 12

REFERENCES

1. Ridpath, John Clark, LL.D-"History of the World"-The Jones Brothers Publishing Co., Cincinnati, O., 1901, Volume II, Book VIII. Chapter XLIV.

2. MacPherson, Dave-The Incredible Cover-Up"-See Ref. (1), Chapter 6.

3. Welch. Robert-"May God Forgive Us"-Henry Regnery Co., Chicago, 1952. Re-published by Belmont Publishing Co. Belmont, Mass. 02178, 1972, as "Again, May God Forgive Us."

See also McCarthy, Sen. Joseph R, "America's Retreat from Victory," Western Islands, Boston & Los Angeles, 1965.

BIBLIOGRAPHIES

Antelman, Rabbi Marvin-"To Eliminate the Opiate" Zahavia, Ltd., 1 East 42nd St., New York 10018, 1974.

Allen, Gary, "Making Plans for a Dictatorship in America," American Opinion magazine, Belmont, Mass. 02178, April, 1971. Allen, Gary "None Dare Call It Conspiracy," Concord Press, Rossmoor, Calif. 1971.

Anonymous "Seventeen Eighty-Nine. An unfinished manuscript which explores the early history of The Communist Conspiracy"-American Opinion, Belmont, Mass. 02178, 1968. Anonymous "The John Franklin Letters"-The Bookmailer, New York, 1959.

Ausabel, Nathan "Pictorial History of the Jewish People"-Crown Publishers, Inc. New York, 1953.

Baxter, Robert-"Narrative of Facts, Characterizing the Supernatural Manifestations in Members of Mr. Irving's Congregation, and Other Individuals, in England and Scotland, and Formerly in the Writer Himself." James Nisbet, London, 1833.

Bennett, Arnold "The Journal of Arnold Bennett, 1896-1928" The Viking Press, New York, 1933. Bernstein, Herman-"The Truth About The Protocols of Zion" Covici-Friede, New York, 1935.

BeVier, William A.-"A Biographical Sketch of C. I. Scofield"-A Thesis Presented to the Faculty of the Graduate School of Southern Methodist University in Partial Fulfillment of the Requirements for the Master of Arts with a Major in History-1960.

Chambers, Roger R.-The Plain Truth About Armstrongism"-Baker Book House, Clark, Doug Amazing Prophecies of the 70's-It's Super K"! Amazing Prophecy Grand Rapids, Mich., 1972. Center, Orange, Calif. 92667, 1975.

Eusebius Pamphilus-"The Ecclesiastical History of Eusebius Pamphilus, Bishop of Cesarea, in Palestine. Translated from the Original with an Introduction by Christian Frederick Cruse"-Baker Book House, Grand Rapids 6, Mich., 1955. Fenton, Fr. Francis "Communism and America's Churches"-American Opinion, Belmont, Mass. 02178.

Festinger, Leon et al.-"When Prophecy Fails"-Harper & Row, New York, 1964. Fitzpatrick, John C.-The Writings of George Washington from the Original Manuscript Sources, 1745-1799"-Prepared under direction of the Washington Bicentennial Commission-Printed June, 1941. U.S. Government Printing Office, Washington, D.C.

Gaebelein, Arno Clemens "Half a Century-The Autobiography of a Servant" Our Hope Publications, 456 Fourth Ave., New York, 1930. Gaebelein, Arno Clemens The Conflict of the Ages" Pryor N. Russell, 1966.

Gaebelein, Arno Clemens "The History of the Scofield Reference Bible," Our Hope Publications, 456 Fourth Ave., New York, 1943. Gannon, Francis X., "Biographical Dictionary of the Left," Western Islands, Boston and Los Angeles, 1973.

Granovsky, Anatoli, "I Was An NKVD Agent," Devin-Adair, 23 E. 26th St., New York, 1962. Pocket edition by Western Islands, Belmont, Mass. 02178, 1987.

Grem, June, "Karl Marx, Capitalist," Enterprise Publications, Inc., P.O. Box 448, Oak Park, Ill. 60303, 1972. Griffin, G. Edward, "The Fearful Master," Western Islands, 395 Concord Ave., Belmont, Mass. 02178, 1964.

Gumaer, David Emerson "Apostasy-The National Council of Churches," American Opinion, Belmont, Mass. 02178, Feb. 1970, pp. 49-68

Hamilton, Frank "The Bible and the Millennium," Rev. Frank Hamilton, 6701 Atlantic Ave., Ventnor, N.J.

Hunter, Edward "The New Drive Against the Anti-Communist Program"-Testimony before the Senate Subcommittee on Internal Security, July 11, 1961.

Laqueur. Walter "A History of Zionism," Holt, Rinehart and Winston, New York, Chicago, San Francisco, 1972. MacPherson, Dave "The Incredible Cover-Up," subtitled, "The True Story On The Pre-Trib Rapture," Logos International, Plainfield. N.J. 07061, 1975 Library of Congress Catalog Card Number 75-25171.

Lipscomb, David "Civil Government" Gospel Advocate Co., Nashville, Tn.. 1957. (Originally published 1866-67) Martin. Rose L.-"Fabian Freeway"-Western Islands, Boston and Los Angeles, 1966. Mason, Alpheus Thomas, "Brandeis-A Free Man's Life" The Viking Press, New York, 1946. McCarthy, Sen. Joseph R.-"America's Retreat from Victory," Western Islands, Boston and Los Angeles, 1965.

Morton, A. L., "The Life and Ideas of Robert Owen," International Publishers, 381 Park Ave. South, New York, 1962 and 1969. Norton, Robert N., M.D. The Restoration of Apostles and Prophets: In the Catholic Apostolic Church"-Bosworth & Harrison, London, 1861. Orwell, George "Nineteen Eighty-Four," Harcourt, Brace & Co., New York, 1949,

Pope Pius XI-"Divini Redemptoris" (Encyclical) 1937.

Pope Pius XI, "Quadragesimo Anno," (Encyclical)-May 15, 1931. Quigley, Carroll-Tragedy and Hope," The Macmillan Co., New York, 1966.

Ridpath, John Clark, LL.D., "History of the World," The Jones Brothers Publishing Co., Cincinnati, Ohio, 1901. Robison, John, A. M., "Proofs of a Conspiracy," George Forman, No. 64 Water St., New York, N.Y., 1798. Re-published by Western Islands, Boston and Los Angeles, 1967.

Sachar, Howard M.-"A History of Israel"-Alfred A. Knopf, New York, 1976.

Sandeen, Ernest R. "The Roots of Fundamentalism"-The University of Chicago Press, 1970.

Spann, Robert L-The Achilles Heel of Conservatism"-Unpublished manuscript, Smithville, Tenn., 1973.

Stormer, John A.-"None Dare Call It Treason"-The Liberty Bell Press, P.O. Box 32, Florissant, Mo., 1964.

Sutton, Antony C., "Wall Street and the Rise of Hitler," '76 Press, Seal Beach, Calif. 90740, 1976.

Toro, Carl-"British Israel"-Unpublished manuscript, Downey, Calif. 90242. Wallace, Foy E., Jr.-"The Christian and the Government," Foy E. Wallace, Jr. Publications, P.O. Box 7410, Ft. Worth, Texas 76111, 1968. Wallace, Foy E., Jr., "God's Prophetic Word," Foy E. Wallace, Jr. Publications, Oklahoma City, 1946. Revised Edition 1960. Wallace, Foy E., Jr., "The Book of Revelation," The Foy E. Wallace, Jr. Publications, P.O. Box 1301, Nashville, Tenn., 1966.

Wallace, Foy E., Jr., "The Sermon on the Mount and the Civil State," Foy E. Wallace, Jr. Publications, P.O. Box 7410, Ft. Worth, Texas 76111, 1967.

Walvoord, John F. and Walvoord, John E., "Armageddon-Oil and the Middle East Crisis," Zondervan Publishing House, Grand Rapids, Mich. 49508, 1974Library of Congress Catalog Card No. 74-4946.

Weizman, Chaim, "Trial and Error," The Weizman Foundation, 1949-Schocken Books, Inc., New York, 1986

Welch. Robert "May God Forgive Us"-Henry Regnery Co., Chicago, 1952. Republished, 1972, as "Again, May God Forgive Us", Belmont Publishing Co.. Belmont, Mass. 02178. Welch. Robert "The Bulletin of the John Birch Society" The John Birch Society Inc., Belmont, Mass. 02178, April, 1972. Welch, Robert "The Neutralizers," The John Birch Society, Belmont, Mass 02178, 1963. Welch, Robert "The Politician"-Belmont Publishing Co., Belmont, Mass. 02178 1964.

Welch, Robert, "The Truth In Time," American Opinion magazine, Belmont, Mass 02178, November, 1966.

Made in United States
Orlando, FL
27 December 2023

41686466R00065